Flannery O'Connor
and the Language of Apocalypse

PRINCETON ESSAYS IN LITERATURE

For a list of titles in this series,
see pages 165-67

Flannery
and the Language

1986

EDWARD KESSLER

O'Connor

of APOCALYPSE

PRINCETON UNIVERSITY PRESS

LIBRARY OF CONGRESS CATALOGING IN PUBLICATION DATA
WILL BE FOUND ON THE LAST PRINTED PAGE OF THIS BOOK

ISBN 0-691-06676-0

PUBLICATION OF THIS BOOK HAS BEEN AIDED BY A GRANT FROM THE
PAUL MELLON FUND OF PRINCETON UNIVERSITY PRESS

THIS BOOK HAS BEEN COMPOSED IN LINOTRON CALEDONIA

CLOTHBOUND EDITIONS OF PRINCETON UNIVERSITY PRESS BOOKS
ARE PRINTED ON ACID-FREE PAPER, AND BINDING MATERIALS ARE
CHOSEN FOR STRENGTH AND DURABILITY

PRINTED IN THE UNITED STATES OF AMERICA
BY PRINCETON UNIVERSITY PRESS
PRINCETON, NEW JERSEY

In memory of two good friends

MARY MOORE MOLONY

and

ROBERT DAVID SALTZ

ACKNOWLEDGMENTS

The College of Arts and Sciences of The American University, through a Mellon grant, made possible my visit to Georgia College.

I wish to thank Gerald Becham and the staff of the Ina Dillard Russell library for their help in investigating The Flannery O'Connor Collection.

I further want to thank individuals who have contributed to my understanding of Flannery O'Connor: Louise Hardeman Abbot, Adrienne Bond, Janet Harrington, and my students in a course on Flannery O'Connor at The American University.

Several other friends and colleagues have read versions of

the manuscript and offered useful comments: Rudolph von Abele, Barry Chabot, Gertrude Dubrovsky, Jay Evans, Doris Grumbach, Jonathan Loesberg, Kermit Moyer, Jo Radner, Jeanne Addison Roberts, Myra Sklarew, and Marion Trousdale.

CONTENTS

Flannery O'Connor
and the Language of Apocalypse

One may be a poet without versing, and a versifier without poetry. —SIDNEY

My God, *my* God, *Thou art a* direct God, *may I not say a* literall God, *a* God *that wouldest bee understood* literally, *and according to the* plaine sense *of all that thou saiest? But thou art also* (Lord *I intend it to thy* glory, *and let no* prophane misinterpreter *abuse it to thy* diminution) *thou art a* figurative, *a* metaphoricall God too. *A* God *in whose words there is such a height of* figures, *such* voyages, *such* peregrinations *to fetch remote and precious* metaphors, *such* extensions, *such* spreadings, *such* Curtaines *of* Allegories, *such* third Heavens of Hyperboles, *so* harmonious eloquutions, *so* retired *and so* reserved expressions, *so* commanding perswasions, *so* perswading commandments, *such sinews even in thy* milke, *and such* things *in thy* words, *as all* prophane Authors, *seeme of the seed of the* Serpent, *that* creepes, *thou art the* Dove, *that flies*. —JOHN DONNE

INTRODUCTION

Flannery O'Connor chose to keep within the boundaries of
fiction, even as she "seemed to contemplate," like her character Mrs. Shortley, "the tremendous frontiers of her true
country." Although some apologists have written as if her
fiction is theology in disguise, her stories a series of illustrations of Grace, O'Connor continually stressed that she was
writing fiction, not religious tracts. Some other commentators have attempted to explain her narratives in terms of her
"real" Southern world, but by now the writer's rejection of
"realism" has become well-known. In either case, the aim
has been to strip her of her various fictional disguises—what
she *seems* to be doing—and to expose the truth behind the

irony, the ambiguity, the paradox. "Many students confuse," she wrote, "the *process* of understanding a thing with understanding it." My aim in the pages that follow is to concentrate on O'Connor's language, the phenomena on the page, and to ignore, for the most part, matters extrinsic to the written text. I hope thereby to reveal a unique metaphoric process that is the writer's means of realizing artistic vision. In disregarding even O'Connor's own interpretations of her work, I would bring to my support a writer she greatly admired, Jacques Maritain:

> Any thesis, whether it profess to demonstrate or to move, is an alien importation in art and as such an impurity. It imposes upon art, in its own sphere, that is to say in the actual production of the work, an alien rule and end; it prevents the work of art issuing from the heart of the artist with the spontaneity of a perfect fruit; it betrays calculation, a dualism between the intelligence of the artist and his sensibility, which the object of art is to have united.[1]

Whereas my theory is very old as a model for reading poetry, it has not been found very useful by recent critics of fiction. The usual objection to Coleridge and the New Critics has been that they do not accommodate the reading of narratives. I hope to show otherwise. By stressing the metaphoric implications across stories, I believe that we can respond to O'Connor more fully, and by setting aside the customary devices of the prose critic (e.g., character, setting, plot), I hope to disclose the poetry inherent in O'Connor's prose, the imaginative world that her configuration of words reveals. My approach may explain, perhaps, why I do not

[1] Jacques Maritain, *Art and Scholasticism: With Other Essays*, trans. J. F. Scanlan (New York: Charles Scribner's Sons, 1943), p. 66.

engage in controversy with critics looking for the standard narrative signals.

Because I see O'Connor in the company of apocalyptic poets like Blake and T. S. Eliot, I do not attend closely to the "materials" of her fiction, the phenomenal reality that seems only a vocabulary for a poetry that aspires to reach beyond both time and space. Her "realism"—her characters' recognizable speech and behavior—resembles the piece of meat that Eliot said the burglar-poet tosses to the watchdog, so that he can go about his business. The outer reality presented seems unreliable, perhaps even misleading, as an entry into the interior life. Like any poet, O'Connor re-creates the world by means of figures of speech that often violate the plain sense of ordinary prose discourse. Representational language could not mirror a hunger that refuses to be satisfied by the food at hand. In an early television interview, O'Connor said that Northerners might appreciate her fiction more readily than Southerners since they would be less distracted by its "accident" (its regional aspects) and would not confuse it with "reality."[2] She continually met with resistance from readers expecting the assurances of verisimilitude: *people aren't like that; things don't happen in that way*. Only through poetic metaphor could she shatter the mirror held up to external nature and declare that fiction is neither true nor false—but fiction.

In calling the reader's attention to O'Connor's use of language, I intend to show how metaphor transforms, if not transfigures, the phenomenon of straightforward, referential prose. Never merely decorative, O'Connor's metaphors constitute verbal strategies for engaging the unknown, for making what Eliot called "raids on the inarticulate." Be-

[2] A print of the Harvey Breit-O'Connor television interview (NBC "Galleyproof," May, 1955) is in the O'Connor Collection at Georgia College.

cause her metaphors are more allied with feeling than with ideas, they sometimes appear, like feelings themselves, illogical, incoherent, and pervasively ambiguous. Therefore I make no attempt to specify meanings for her metaphors but instead aim to show how they work to set forth meanings. Any figure of speech can be read referentially or rhetorically, and we must keep aware of the necessary distinction before we can appreciate the momentary reconciliations that O'Connor sometimes achieves, particularly in her later fiction. In alienating her readers from the world they already know, she offers them in metaphor not a copy but an imitation, in the classical sense: whereas a copy represents and is consequently subordinate to the already made, an imitation re-creates, joining man's creating power with the creating power of nature. Rather than demonstrating a preconceived "truth," O'Connor's stories show that contriving a fiction and discovering a truth are not antithetical.

Because language exists in time, its reconciliations must be temporal, and though believing in the final reconciliation that religion provides, O'Connor nevertheless knew that her "true country" could be seen only from the threshold where metaphor has its being: looking backward at the given world while at the same time looking beyond it. As with Blake, belief, in any theological sense, appears in the work as a way of *seeing* and manifests itself obliquely. It is metaphor that informs the work and only on those rare occasions when O'Connor resorts to direct statement (e.g., when she identifies the Displaced Person with Christ or a waterstain with the Holy Ghost) does she weaken her fictional contract. To argue that her stories proclaim dogmatic beliefs is to ignore the equivocal nature of metaphor, in effect to deny its invigorating power and to arrest the process of language whereby belief is in the making. Metaphor as lie—the bringing together of two incongruous entities *as if* they were one—remains the poet's only means of pointing toward the true, and in O'Connor's act of writing fiction, it supersedes all other shapes for human experience:

> The *Geist* is "there" not as a thing, a stone, an animal, a statue, or a hero, but as a *Self*. This implies that its historical manifestation too must die so that the community has to become the true "body of Christ." In this way, the two dimensions of "representation" in Christianity—historicity and community—have also to be substantiated *and* overcome. Religion, then, is the place where the manifestation of the Spirit and the death of its representation may be seen.[3]

What religion presents cannot be represented, as Paul Ricoeur asserts—and even his "place" is a metaphor. O'Connor's subordination of both history and community to metaphor may imply her acceptance of the impossibility of representing "true reconciliation." Because O'Connor's "history" is inward and her authentic community figurative, her violent metaphors paradoxically deny her readers social adjustment and stability while at the same time opening up the possibility of transcending the limitations of conventional social and verbal forms.

O'Connor's noted satire and irony, moreover, are less dependent on moral norms external to her fiction than on her compelling need to rescue her readers from a closed linguistic order. When metaphor hardens into cliché or into concept, it no longer retains its power to evolve a new consciousness. Showing how satisfaction with an accepted lan-

---

[3] Paul Ricoeur, "Biblical Hermeneutics," *Semia: An Experimental Journal for Biblical Criticism*, 4 (1975), p. 141.

guage parallels self-satisfaction, O'Connor ridicules the platitudes that block her characters from any genuine understanding of themselves. She wrote to a friend: "I doubtless hate pious language worse than you because I believe the realities it hides." By exposing counterfeit speech, the author begins the process that eventually brings to life the hidden, unacknowledged self. Both her irony and her satire are consequently not directed, as in the eighteenth century, at affirming a known, established order external to the fiction, but at displacing it. Rather than inviting her readers to join in a conspiracy against her characters, a conspiracy of intelligence and good taste (as perhaps Flaubert does), she makes them realize that a stock language limits all of us to stock responses. On the other hand, we are reminded that every dead metaphor or cliché masks a genuine emotion that can be awakened. In "The Comforts of Home," Thomas knows that even though his mother's "conversation moved from cliché to cliché there were real experiences behind them." Irony exposes both vulgarity and banality, in the interest of liberating our "real experiences."

Because metaphor is a way of seeing, and not the object seen, we can detect O'Connor's world-view in how her characters react to their surroundings. Many of them possess what Blake called "single vision"; they see objectively, that is, only what meets the eye. They take the world and language at face value. For example, Mrs. Flood in *Wise Blood*, who "took every word at face value," cannot comprehend the meaning that Hazel Motes' life is figuring forth:

"I'm not clean," he said.
She stood staring at him, unmindful of the broken dishes at her feet. "I know it," she said after a minute,

"you got blood on your nightshirt and on the bed. You ought to get you a washwoman . . ."

"That's not the kind of clean," he said.

Motes tells her that "if there's no bottom in your eyes, they hold more." But a true literalist of the imagination, she comprehends nothing of what he says: "The landlady stared a long time, seeing nothing at all." Perhaps worse off is a character like Hulga in "Good Country People" who has "the look of someone who has achieved blindness by an act of will and means to keep it." She ignores her natural surroundings, the ground of metaphor, and therefore suffers a blindness more profound than Mrs. Flood's:

> "We are all damned," she said, "but some of us have taken off our blindfolds, and see that there's nothing to see. It's a kind of salvation."

O'Connor's intolerance of dead metaphors probably influenced as well her attitude toward genre, preordained literary forms. The poets Robert Lowell and Elizabeth Bishop claimed O'Connor as one of their own, and she herself praised Hawthorne for attempting to steer the novel "in the direction of poetry." By displacing history and community as primary subjects for fiction, and disparaging "social or economic or psychological forces," she chose to elevate poetic metaphor beyond its usual position in customary prose. As a consequence, the interplay of ways of seeing overrides the beginning-middle-end of conventional form. She could easily begin a novel by presenting a character in an unstable situation, and she could remove that instability through the intervention of an outside force, but she struggled to create sustaining middles. She wrote to Caroline Gordon: "I am doing the whole middle section of the novel over. The beginning and the end suit me, but that middle is bad. It isn't dramatic enough. I telescoped that middle section so as to get on with the end, but now that I've got the end, I see there isn't enough middle. . . ." A metaphor, of course, maintains no middle. Perhaps both *Wise Blood* and *The Violent Bear it Away* lack effective middles because we realize that plot and character are secondary. We await the consummation of the author's informing metaphors. Her acknowledged difficulty in completing both very short novels probably came about because she was inventing not an action but a delaying action. As in the story of Job, the middles of her longer narratives seem in retrospect to disappear. We remember her voices for metaphor, Hazel Motes and Tarwater, but tend to cast aside Enoch Emory and Rayber who distract us from the controlling movement.

Much closer to poetry in its condensation, the short story remained O'Connor's congenial form. Its single moment made possible her escape from the trap of time, the cause and effect of conventional narrative, and allowed her to assume a position from which initial action and denouement connect, necessitating little intermediate traffic with the quotidian. Resembling the Biblical parable, the short story intimately combines narrative with a metaphorical process. Thus any single metaphor is a microcosm: the ever-present, ever-varying conjunction of the known and unknown.

In describing Coleridge's "doctrines" of imagination, I. A. Richards could well have been talking about Flannery O'Connor, who shares the poet's discoveries about the natural world and about himself:

1. The mind of the poet at moments, penetrating "the film of familiarity and selfish solicitude," gains an

insight into reality, reads Nature as a symbol of something behind or within Nature not ordinarily perceived.

2. The mind of the poet creates a Nature into which his own feelings, his aspirations and apprehensions, are projected.[4]

Although both writers project a world of words, within which they can read and know themselves, they also apprehend a power external to the self that provides the cure for solipsism. For both Coleridge and O'Connor the "something" behind or within nature should more accurately be labeled a "someone" or a "presence," to use her recurring word. All self-comforting fictions dissolve when one is alone on a wide wide sea, isolated from "ordinary sights." Only by separating the eye from its familiar objects can the poet, in the words of old Tarwater, "BURN YOUR EYES CLEAN."

O'Connor's metaphors are rarely simple resemblances (or compressed similes) that connect us with the natural order. They both rescue us from things as they are, and free us from the confines of "ordinary" discourse. Just as her early protagonist, Hazel Motes, realizes that "if there's no bottom in your eyes, they hold more," her later hero, Tarwater, realizes that his stomach also has no bottom: "the bottom split out of his stomach so that nothing would heal or fill it but the bread of life." Figurative language is the poet's only evidence of things not seen, her only promise of "redemption" for her suffering characters, who, like most people, resist having to endure the birth-agony of a new consciousness. Flannery O'Connor's characters develop *in spite* of themselves, for to see what resides "behind or within" nature re-

[4] I. A. Richards, *Coleridge on Imagination* (Bloomington: Indiana University Press, 1960), p. 145.

quires painful displacement from the material world, and from *words* as they correspond to *things*. In *The Violent Bear it Away*, Tarwater would ignore the process of his interior life and substitute a mere objective existence:

> He tried when possible to pass over these thoughts, to keep his vision located on an even level, to see no more than what was in front of his face and to let his eyes stop at the surface of that. It was as if he were afraid that if he let his eye rest for an instant longer than was needed to place something—a spade, a hoe, the mule's hind quarters before his plow, the red furrow under him—that the thing would suddenly stand before him, strange and terrifying, demanding that he name it and name it justly and be judged for the name he gave it. He did all he could to avoid the threatened intimacy of creation.

Projecting one world while revealing another, O'Connor would turn her reluctant hero into original man, naming the things of God's creation. However, after his fall, he must painfully *reenter* the originating metaphoric process that refuses to allow things, even a spade or a hoe, to remain unspirited. In effect, Tarwater's thoughts mirror O'Connor's personal struggle with a literal or representational language that accompanies the understanding. Her metaphoric language, on the other hand, was her means of sharing the mysterious and threatening "intimacy of creation." As with Blake, Coleridge, Eliot, in their differing ways, creative power can make the already-made terrifying, a threat to the established selfhood. "Human kind / Cannot bear very much reality."

The Devil's voice in *The Violent Bear it Away* warns that "nobody can do two things without straining themselves," but in the following essay I hope to demonstrate how O'Connor's metaphors consistently do two things, with a minimum of strain: intensifying our awareness of creating nature while, through the "darkness of parable," opening up a way beyond the world, a "presence" external to words.

After describing O'Connor's distinctive approach to poetic metaphor (with some discussion of two particular examples) I focus on her special linguistic device for achieving her momentary reconciliation of opposites: the *as if* construction, which coalesces a utilitarian prose by which we "see no more than what is in front of [our] face" and a figurative poetry that promises us all that we have never seen. The *as if* remains, both early and late, O'Connor's poetic signature, her means of engaging "mystery," that unknown power that cannot be grasped by the understanding alone.

The third section of my essay considers some of the difficulties that a writer faces when attempting to represent mystery, particularly the mystery of evil, in action. I contend that O'Connor is far more successful in presenting the good because, like the metaphoric process itself, it is organic, "always under construction." Mystery was her name for the potent force behind phenomena, the energy behind and within each story which, like the stories themselves, can never be fully explained, only witnessed.

Finally, I describe some of O'Connor's difficulties in making ends for her various narratives. From the beginning, she rejected the causality of customary fiction as an ordering principle; she continually sought the cause of cause-and-effect, and as a consequence, she had to forgo the usual ends of traditional narrative (e.g., secular justice, fulfillment in another, career success) and other temporary satisfactions attending the physical world. Denying that the here and now have ultimate significance, O'Connor accepted the priority of spiritual evolution over art, and therefore she realized that narrative can never generate its own end. Refusing to view fiction as a riddle to be solved or a box to be snapped shut at the end, she struggled to create satisfying endings that yet do not foreclose possibility. Although she acknowledged that fiction should not state meaning but reveal it, nevertheless she sometimes had difficulty in effecting a reconciliation between a statement that delivers and a metaphor that only promises. Perhaps Caroline Gordon's advice that O'Connor "elevate" her endings finally proves questionable or, perhaps, O'Connor misunderstood precisely what her mentor wanted. O'Connor wrote of "The Artificial Nigger":

> I wrote that story a good many times, having a lot of trouble with the end. I frequently send my stories to Mrs. Tate and she is always telling me that the endings are too flat and that at the end I must gain some altitude and get a larger view.

After creating a highly satisfactory metaphoric close for "The Artificial Nigger," one that reveals beauty, the mysterious power within man and the natural world, O'Connor uncharacteristically weakened her resolution by a paragraph of direct assertion, and furthermore, again uncharacteristically, she violated her character's mental sanctity, with phrases such as "he knew" and "he understood":

> He had never thought himself a great sinner before but he saw now that his true depravity had been hidden from him lest it cause him despair. He realized that he was forgiven for his sins. . . . He saw that no sin was too monstrous for him to claim as his own. . . .

O'Connor momentarily replaced her customary metaphoric

design on the world with direct commentary that counter-
acts the power of her own revelation. By confronting her
rare unhappy juxtaposition of two language modes, we can
more happily celebrate the consummate endings of other
stories such as "Everything That Rises Must Converge" and
"Revelation." Although Flannery O'Connor, like John
Donne, may have praised a *direct* and *literal* God who
speaks *plain sense*, she was chosen by Donne's metaphoric
God in whose words there is a "height of *figures*." Her language of apocalypse discloses the life that survives all aesthetic ends.

Note. The reader familiar with the O'Connor critical ter-
rain may be surprised by my limited use of the substantial
body of illuminating studies now available. Although I have
surveyed most of it—and probably learned more than I acknowledge—I choose to deal with O'Connor's fiction in a
first-hand way. I assume a general familiarity with O'Connor's work on the reader's part and do not attempt full and
original "readings" of the stories. So many critical works exist, beginning in the late sixties, accumulating substantially
in the seventies, and continuing to our own day, that I hes-
itate to single out particular approaches. However, a very
recent book by Frederick Asals, *Flannery O'Connor: The
Imagination of Extremity* (1982) does appear to sanction
what I have done. Although Professor Asals' concerns are
primarily thematic in terms of the polarities that constitute
O'Connor's various works, he nevertheless asserts "the
tendency of the metaphoric activity in Flannery O'Connor's
later fiction" as well as noting that the early "*Wise Blood* is
a genuinely sustained performance, its unity gained from
the images, symbols, and motifs that flow outward from its

hero rather than from a conventionally well made plot." I would describe that "metaphoric activity" more fully, showing how O'Connor's "tendency" has been realized.

I acknowledge two books as central to the theoretical concerns of my study: Paul Ricoeur's *The Rule of Metaphor* and Hans Vaihinger's *The Philosophy of "As If."* They have nothing directly to do with Flannery O'Connor, but in significant ways both aided me in dealing with her.

Because the body of O'Connor's work is small, I have not cluttered the text with citations to the primary texts: the *Collected Stories*, the two short novels *Wise Blood* and *The Violent Bear it Away*, and Sally Fitzgerald's collection of letters, *The Habit of Being*. I assume that readers of my essay have met Flannery O'Connor and need not be introduced.

I

THE VIOLENCE OF
METAPHOR

Even though interpretation demands that we limit textual meaning, the direction of the interpretive movement can be questioned: away from language toward extrinsic knowledge, of whatever sort, or deeper into the labyrinth of words? Believing that language possesses its own reality, I intend to follow, in O'Connor's phrase, "words moving secretly toward some goal of their own." Her metaphors are rarely simple resemblances or satisfying correspondences between man and a natural order, as those of Eudora Welty and Wallace Stevens often are. An apocalyptic poet like T. S. Eliot, O'Connor finds limited value in analogies with the physical world and aspires to "rise" beyond the limits of time and space. Both Eliot and O'Connor are unsatisfied by the relative ends of experience or by momentary pleasures, and acknowledge that "Love is most nearly itself / When here and now cease to matter." Whereas the language of Welty and Stevens refreshes what we already know, O'Connor and Eliot create metaphors of displacement or estrangement that make way for the "revelation" of a new world.

The mythical fall becomes, for O'Connor, a fall into the literal, where things *are* but do not *seem*. The phenomenal world entertains a power and a presence frequently undetected by O'Connor's characters whose pride distorts their vision, and even determines the very language they use. For instance, in "The Artificial Nigger," Mr. Head claims a "calm understanding of life" and a "will and strong character" that enable him to "guide" others through the world. But in the story's initial paragraph, O'Connor disturbs Mr. Head's hold on experience by evoking, through metaphor, not what is, but what could be:

Mr. Head awakened to discover that the room was full of moonlight. He sat up and stared at the floor boards—the color of silver—and then at the ticking on his pillow, which might have been brocade, and after a second he saw half of the moon five feet away in his shaving mirror, paused as if it were waiting his permission to enter. It rolled forward and cast a dignifying light on everything. The straight chair against the wall looked stiff and attentive as if it were awaiting an order and Mr. Head's trousers, hanging to the back of it, had an almost noble air, like the garment some great man had just flung to his servant; but the face on the moon was a grave one. It gazed across the room and out the window where it floated over the horse stall and appeared to contemplate itself with the look of a young man who sees his old age before him.

In this densely figurative opening, O'Connor shares with the reader the possibilities that the understanding may ignore. Mr. Head stares at the floor boards and the ticking, but to him they are only things, mere objects, without the "dignifying light" of metaphor which can redeem things from their ordinariness. In this early-morning scene, things are poised on the threshold, waiting to be metamorphosed, to be *permitted* to assume significance. Things "almost" have dignity, but the metaphoric process is incomplete. O'Connor's *as if* announces a suspended presence that Mr. Head with his "single vision" cannot as yet recognize. O'Connor's *as if* copula, which we will look at more fully later on, signals that mere resemblance—the floor boards that resemble silver—cannot bring about a radical change in how we see. Simile can intensify our awareness of the given world, but it does not, like O'Connor's *as if*, yoke together unambiguous declarative sentences with metaphoric uncertainty. Like metaphor, *as if* acts as a hinge connecting things as they are with things as they could or might be. Mr. Head sees only half the moon in his shaving mirror, only the *base* of metaphor, but he is unaware of his deficient vision, unconscious that he possesses the power to change his life. The moon-imagination stands ready to be welcomed into his house and life, but Mr. Head's dormant imaginative power will be made active only later, after he has recognized his own essential displacement, visible in the face of the child he has attempted to guide:

The child was standing about ten feet away, his face bloodless under the gray hat. His eyes were triumphantly cold. There was no light in them, no feeling, no interest. He was merely there, a small figure, waiting. Home was nothing to him.

After confronting the negative face of metaphor, Mr. Head and the child Nelson discover its positive face: the Artificial Nigger, embodying the power and presence that can transfigure human nature.

Almost immediately after the highly figurative opening of "The Artificial Nigger," O'Connor introduces another kind of language, a straightforward, unenlightened descriptive prose that represents the raw material (the "facts" of discourse) that the "miraculous moonlight" (the poet's metaphor) works upon:

> He sat up and grasped the iron posts at the foot of his bed and raised himself until he could see the face of the alarm clock which sat on an overturned bucket beside the chair. The hour was two in the morning. The alarm on the clock did not work but he was not dependent on any mechanical means to awaken him. Sixty years had not dulled his responses; his physical reactions, like his moral ones, were guided by his will and strong character, and these could be seen plainly in his features.

In her opening paragraph O'Connor rejects mere description and provides instead a dramatic engagement between poetic metaphor and declarative prose, whose end is to heighten disparity, two kinds of language seeking an accommodation. Moreover, the disjunction between the author's insight into uncertainty and her character's blindness to everything but his own positivism creates a meaningful rift. O'Connor's "poetry" is, therefore, openly impure; instead of aspiring, like the symbolist poets, to the condition of music, she accepts the interdependence of prose and poetry, of logical discourse and imaginative, expressive language.

In the second quoted paragraph, straightforward prose is again threatened, this time not by metaphor but by irony. Beginning with what appears to be disinterested description, the author gradually undermines the truth of her own representation. Mr. Head believes that "sixty years had not dulled his responses," but the opening paragraph of the story demonstrates that they are indeed sorely limited. The author unmasks Mr. Head's assessment of his strong will and character: they are what he *thinks* he sees, not what the reader sees and will see exposed as the story proceeds. Mr. Head's ability to order experience through his strong will or through his willful language remains suspect throughout. To be ignorant of metaphor (and irony) partakes of the ignorance which is death.

Those opposites by means of which we impose order on verbal experience—imagination versus rationality; expressive language versus logical discourse; metaphor versus declarative concrete sentences; poetry versus prose—are themselves false if seen as an unbridgeable duality. What Donne called the *direct* and *literal* God is also, at the same time, a *figurative* and *metaphorical* God. When O'Connor disrupts our sense of discrete categories she changes how we relate to language and consequently how we relate to the world. The violence of O'Connor's metaphors, like Donne's, aims at creating a rift, an avenue between extremes. The incompatibility of some of her figures with the context in which they appear testifies to an extravagance necessary in order to keep words from becoming dead things, to keep language from becoming merely a mirror of ordinary experience, a confining rather than a liberating form. Like her character Tarwater, O'Connor has a desperate hunger for the absolute and thus, for her, meaning can never be *identified* with shifting words; it is only *released* whenever words engage, conflict with, and oppose deadening cliché.

In contrast to O'Connor's use of violent metaphors to displace us from earthly satisfaction *as an end* and to compel us to enter a renovated world, Eudora Welty uses figurative language to make us more at home in the world, and thus her customary mode is analogy, resemblance, rather than the disruptive metaphors we discover in most O'Connor stories. Technically, simile, rather than metaphor, is Welty's characteristic figure since the terms of comparison remain distinct yet compatible, mirroring man's familiarity with his surroundings: both the social and the natural world. In a way, Welty's figures extend a subject horizontally; that is, they welcome man to the satisfactions inherent in time and space, but sometimes, like ships dragging anchor, they create a language drift that points toward spiritual drifting, a contentment with relative satisfactions, without any compelling need for an absolute. Welty shares with Wallace Stevens not only her affinity with resemblances but also her belief that there is no such thing as *the* truth. Thus her metaphoric excursions always return home, reinforcing the satisfactions that are at hand. A few illustrations from Welty's fiction may serve to highlight her fundamentally different use of figurative language.

Sometimes Welty's similes seem to forget the purpose they serve, as in the opening of her story "The Whistle" (I have divided with slashes and numbered the modifications of her extended similes):

Night fell. The darkness was thin / like some sleazy dress [1] / that had been worn for many winters [2] / and al-

[3]ways lets the cold through / to the[4] bones. Then the moon rose. A farm lay quite visible, / like a white[1] stone / in wa[2]ter, / among[3] the stretches of deep woods / in their colorless[4] dead leaf.

Or a similar elaboration from another early story:

. . . like a[1] fish / he had[2] spied / just below the[3] top of the water / in a sunny[4] lake / in the[5] country / when he[6] was a child.

These "horizontal" extensions are perhaps extreme but they are not uncharacteristic. The comparisons assume a life of their own, and many times we are left with language that is admirably decorative, but perhaps not essential. The vehicle of metaphor often abandons its tenor as it proceeds. We witness a chain reaction, without O'Connor's apocalyptic bang at the end. (Welty's descriptive detail can likewise qualify a subject until it almost disappears, as in this from *Delta Wedding*: "Very quietly out front, on the high and sloping porch, standing and sitting on the railing between the four remembered pale, square cypress posts, was stationed a crowd of people, dressed darkly, but vaguely powdered over with gold dust of their thick arrival here in midafternoon.") In contrast to Welty's extensions, O'Connor's uncharacteristic similes usually complete themselves in a limited and immediate fashion; the complement of *like* or *as* being frequently a single entity. Similes add momentary clarifications that are always subordinate to the energetic metaphoric process moving toward a revelation and an end. O'Connor's noted directness denies her those resemblances that are merely entertaining or pleasurable: "Mr. Head looked like an ancient child and Nelson like a miniature old man." Elaboration retards the process of which resemblance is a necessary but minor part. O'Connor wrote: "I am not one of the subtle sensitive writers like Eudora Welty. I see only what is outside and what sticks out a mile, such things as the sun that nobody has to uncover or be bright to see."

O'Connor's aversion to the making of extensive resemblances brings her more into the company of T. S. Eliot than of Eudora Welty and Wallace Stevens, both of whom resemble Narcissus, seeking to discover himself in the pool of nature. In an essay, "Three Academic Pieces," Stevens would counter Narcissus' bad reputation as a self-centered materialist. He contends that the poet looks for himself within the pool of nature, and in language, another reflecting pool. He could be speaking for Welty as well as for himself: ". . . if it were possible to look into the sea as into glass and if we should do so and suddenly should behold there some extraordinary transfiguration of ourselves, the experience would strike us as one of those amiable revelations that nature occasionally vouchsafes to favorites." The two words that Stevens reiterates in his essay—*resemblance* and *pleasure*—exclude any need for an absolute, any threat to the self that could possibly disrupt the pool and make it unreflective. In "Clytie" Welty appears to recognize that resemblances can lead to no meaningful end, or as for Narcissus, to a death without significance. Welty says of Clytie: "It was purely for a resemblance to a vision that she examined the secret, mysterious, unrepeated faces she met in the street of Farr's Gin." Her search to find a resemblance, a complement, is a doomed venture without a controlling order. What could be a poet's delightful entertainment becomes for Clytie a series of analogies that does not conclude but merely stops. Like Narcissus, she finds herself reflected in water (in her case, the waters of a rain barrel) and dies.

This early, O'Connor-like use of violence disappears from Welty's fiction as it develops. More often, Welty uses her figurative language to effect harmony between man and nature, and it serves equally to relate individuals to their communities and to their pasts, providing a fuller context for self-integration. In her later *The Optimist's Daughter*, the characteristic resemblances unite people with each other and even with the dead:

> The procession passed between ironwork gates whose kneeling angels and looping vines shone black *as* licorice. The top of the hill ahead was crowded with winged angels and lifesized effigies of bygone *citizens* in old fashioned dress, standing *as if* by count among the columns and shafts and conifers *like* a *familiar* set of passengers collected on deck of a ship, on which they *all knew each other*—bona-fide *members* of a small local excursion, embarked on a voyage that is *always returning* in dreams [my emphasis].

The similes make the familiar more familiar, and the "as if" does not, as in O'Connor, invite an unknown that can often destroy our sense of well-being. Whereas O'Connor's violent metaphors voyage beyond a given world, Welty's metaphoric excursion is *always returning*. Welty's figures produce, in Stevens's words, "amiable revelations."

Readers who find Welty's method charming are likely to be offended by O'Connor's deliberately discomforting vision. O'Connor's "like" and "as" often evoke unpleasing resemblances, especially in her early work when she seems to share Eliot's (also early) *contemptus mundi*. Both writers need to degrade the vehicle of metaphor in order to express their dissatisfaction with superficial beauty, to alert society to its spiritual poverty, what Eliot calls "The thousand sordid images / Of which your soul was constituted." When Hazel Motes meets the prostitute Mrs. Watts, in *Wise Blood*, "His throat got drier and his heart began to grip him like a little ape clutching the bars of its cage." And when Mrs. Watts smiles her "grin was as curved and sharp as the blade of a sickle." These dehumanizing resemblances serve, obliquely, to declare, in the words of one of O'Connor's titles, that "the world is almost rotten." Even words themselves can be ugly when they remind us of what we are not: "The ugly words settled in Mr. Shiftlet's head like a group of buzzards in the top of a tree." O'Connor was quite aware that she had "cultivated the ugly," and her very limited use of simile indicates that she, like Eliot, could not be satisfied by earthly resemblances. Metaphor, in its denial of a referential function, became these artists' means of projecting their overpowering visionary world. Eliot once declared that he wanted "to get *beyond poetry*," finally to create a "poetry so transparent that in reading it we are intent on what the poem *points at*, and not on the poetry. . . ."[1] Of course, language can never be transparent but at best translucent; however, by their metaphors of displacement Eliot and O'Connor struggled to prove that there is both something to see and something to see beyond.

By looking at two of O'Connor's recurring words, one drawn from external nature ("place") and one from human nature ("smiles") we can perhaps witness how the author transforms simple representation into metaphor. Like other Southern writers, O'Connor stressed in occasional essays the importance of geographical place for a writer; however, in her fiction we find that the word does not remain long on the literal, denotative level. Her use of "smiles" further em-

[1] Quoted in F. O. Matthiessen, *The Achievement of T. S. Eliot* (New York: Oxford University Press, 1958), p. 90.

phasizes her dissatisfaction with any descriptive detail that we accept at *face* value. Images *in themselves* are deceptive and like any phenomenon they conceal as much as they reveal. They assume their true life (and value) only when seen as parts of an organic process whose end remains outside of the process itself.

When accused of being "morally confused," Rufus Johnson (in "The Lame Shall Enter First") screams: "I lie and steal because I'm good at it"; and when Flannery O'Connor was asked why she wrote fiction, she used the same words: "I write because I'm good at it." Her kinship with Rufus might be extended: "I lie, i.e., I create fictions; and I steal, i.e., I appropriate from my environment my material for fiction." It is unlikely that any American writer, Faulkner included, has so successfully stolen the idiom of a region, but the significance of "place" in O'Connor's work has surely been overstressed, if not misunderstood, by Southern commentators wishing to claim her for their own. The word "place" does not summon up a static picture, but a dynamic metaphor. As it accumulates meaning in its various contexts we find that the word ultimately has little to do with Baldwin County, Georgia. As Melville said of Queequeg's birthplace, "It is not down in any map. True places never are." Often in O'Connor's stories, associating oneself with a place produces a false security, an illusion of permanence which must inevitably be shattered. Misguided O'Connor characters try to fix themselves in time and particularly in space, without realizing what she calls "our essential displacement." Unlike the Agrarians, O'Connor did not long for some closed, static, hierarchical society, but saw the writer as one who "operates at a peculiar crossroads where time and place and eternity somehow meet. The writer's problem is to find that location." In its various uses, the word "place" refers to conditions of being, having minimal correspondence with geography. No matter how vividly represented, "place" serves as a metaphoric means. O'Connor declared: "I don't consider that I write *about* the South."

In "A Circle in the Fire," Mrs. Cope is proud that she has "the best kept place in the country," and more proud that she "had to work to save the place and work to keep it." Ironically, O'Connor encloses this pastoral world with a "wall of trees" that becomes, in turn, "granite" and a "fortress." The threat to Mrs. Cope's established order assumes various forms and disguises: nutgrass, fire, hurricane, totalitarian forces, ineffectual Negroes, a released bull—and the boys, led by one named Powell, who come to the farm for a visit. The conflict between Mrs. Cope and the reckless boys who eventually set fire to the "sentinel line of trees" focuses the events of "A Circle in the Fire," but the story's meaning heavily depends on the metaphor of place. Mrs. Cope, unimaginative, clinging to the "fact" of ownership, seeks through willful assertion to deny the power of the unknown: "I've had to work to save this place and work to keep it" and "this is my place." Even Mrs. Cope's ignorant farm woman, Mrs. Pritchard, realizes that there are forces beyond her control. To Mrs. Cope's cliché, "I'll take it as it comes," she responds: "[What] if it all come at oncet sometime." Conscious of her vulnerability, Mrs. Pritchard can imagine the absence, hence the insubstantiality, of "place": "Mrs. Pritchard folded her arms and gazed down the road as if she could easily enough see all those fine hills flattened to nothing."

The serpent that enters Mrs. Cope's garden of Eden is the young boy Powell, who had lived on the farm for a short period before being displaced. At first hand, he has learned the futility of relying on physical permanence. However, he maintains his lost Eden in his mind, so that in returning, he can relate the imagined to the real, i.e., the *real* estate he is being expelled from for the second time. One of Powell's cronies says, "he ain't satisfied with where he's at except this place here." Rather than trying to effect some harmony between image and idea, Powell chooses to destroy the physical base of his mental image, in the hope of eliminating his need for significance. Whether a satanic nihilist, a prophet of the apocalypse, or a mystic seeking some unmediated vision, Powell, unlike Mrs. Cope, lives in two realms simultaneously. When he decides to act, he resembles "a ghost sprung upright in his coffin. 'If this place was not here any more,' he said, 'you would never have to think of it again.' "

The irony declares, of course, that imaginary places are indestructible; they feed on absence, grow more intense with actual loss. Released from the army, Hazel Motes in *Wise Blood* returns to his home, Eastrod: "Eastrod filled his head and then went out beyond and filled the space that stretched from the train across the empty darkening fields." When he finds the town gone, his house a skeleton, he begins his doomed quest to find an earthly replacement. In this early work, O'Connor foreshadows the encounter between literal and metaphoric thinking in "A Circle in the Fire," but the results differ profoundly. Several people in *Wise Blood* try to bind Hazel Motes to place, but he fights to keep moving, and ironically he trusts his automobile to provide his means of escaping materialism. When he finally blinds himself, severing his connection with any visible place, he yearns to recreate a permanent Eastrod in his imagination. He takes walks without any destination and when he can no longer fabricate an earthly goal, he retreats to his room, where he walks "in one spot, moving his feet up and down." *Moving in place* suggests the limited range O'Connor found in her metaphor at this time. When Hazel Motes dies, he escapes not only the world, the flesh, and the devil, but also the landlady who embodies them all. In harmony with the devil in *The Violent Bear it Away* (who tells Tarwater: "you're left by yourself in an empty place"), she says, "The world is an empty place," and "Nobody ought to be without a place of their own to be and I'm willing to give you a home here with me, a place where you can always stay." Finally she burlesques the metaphor: "I got a place for you in my heart." In O'Connor's early engagement of metaphoric and representational language, "place" finds its material dead end in sentimentality and cliché.

In the later "A Circle in the Fire," O'Connor has deepened and complicated her metaphor. Whereas earlier we found no coming together of ways of seeing, no interpretation of material and imaginative place, we now discover a vital development, not a withheld possibility but a symbolic realization. When Powell and his friends set the fire, O'Connor describes the effect of actual destruction on the invincible Mrs. Cope, but more emphatically on her young daughter. The fire spreads and, agents of an anonymous power, "the boys disappeared shrieking behind it." The child realizes the inadequacy of physical place and experiences the superior power that acts only in or through place. Clearly both the *felt* misery and the *felt* meaning cannot be directly represented, but they can be evoked through metaphorical language, particularly by O'Connor's characteristic *as if*:

> The child came to a stop beside her mother and stared up at her face *as if* she had never seen it before. It was

the face of the new misery she *felt*, but on her mother it looked old and it looked *as if* it might have belonged to anybody, a Negro or a European or to Powell himself. The child turned her head quickly and past the Negroes' ambling figures she could see the column of smoke rising and widening unchecked inside the granite line of trees. She stood taut, listening, and could just catch in the distance a few wild high shrieks of joy *as if* the prophets were dancing in the fiery furnace, in the circle the angel had cleared for them [my emphasis].

Here, as elsewhere, particularly in "The Artificial Nigger," O'Connor conceives of metaphor as a means of destroying one order of perception (the referential) and replacing it by imaginative vision—and *feeling*. Moreover, her metaphors do not *substitute* a more familiar term for the one displaced in the metaphorical contract. By diverting the current running between the two poles of metaphor, she discovers what lies hidden beneath both language and the world. The child must reassess what she has known, and her feeling of dislocation, her misery, takes form in her mother's face, which grows *unfamiliar* as it joins a "felt" or imagined family, beyond the boundaries of existing society and prosaic language. Smug satisfaction with one's place and self—for O'Connor asserted that place is "inside as well as outside"— produces comforting analogies with our surroundings or reproduces itself as cliché. But metaphor abides no representational middle ground between what we claim to be and what we could be. The new misery "might have belonged to anybody," but it finds its immediate home in Mrs. Cope. The final metaphor, comparing the boys to the Daniel-like figures in the Prophecy, is not a key to a consistent allegory

but only another means of extending place, this time backward to a mythic community. Anxiety before the unknown,
whether in or outside a text, causes some of O'Connor's
readers to retreat to assuring explanations of mysteries
based on Christian history or on the writer's personal history. But the *words* are the only access to fictional meaning,
although they can never be *identified* with meaning. The
word "place," for example, does not possess denotation,
neither is it finally an image. O'Connor's metaphor tells us
that a change has occurred, but the change takes effect only
if the reader permits it to. As Augustine wrote: "Even if
Moses himself appeared to us and said, 'This is what I
meant,' we should not actually see that he meant it but
should take his word for it."[2]

Like O'Connor's other metaphors, place discloses and
deepens its meanings in the course of her writing career. In
her first published story, "The Geranium," a Southerner,
transplanted to the North, feels "trapped in this place" and
he longs to return to the "good place" he came from. And
very shortly, Hazel Motes in *Wise Blood* will be denied his
home place and find himself in a Pullman berth that, in his
imagination, becomes a coffin, a final place that is inescapable. Motes's longing for his familial home may resemble
O'Connor's homesickness, whether in Iowa or New York.
However, later, in recalling her "necessary" return to the
South when she became ill, she was not elated. Responding
to a friend's complaint about the possibility of having to
come back home, O'Connor sounds sharp: "You get no con-
dolences from me. This is a return I have faced and when I
faced it I was roped and tied and resigned the way it is necessary to be resigned to death. . . ." Her association of place

[2] Augustine, *The Confessions*, trans. F. J. Sheed (London: Sheed and Ward,
1943), Book XII, xxv, p. 295.

with death indicates the negative aspect of her metaphor, which will find its balancing affirmative power only after she has cultivated the place "inside." The writer eventually overcame her fears of being trapped in a place, once the place became, in her words, "diluted with time and matter." In order to be recreated in the mind, actual place has to be dissolved—or burned away, to use the stronger metaphor of "A Circle in the Fire" and *The Violent Bear it Away*. Metaphor became her escape from the limitations of both place and time, because, as George Steiner says, even though language happens in time, it also "very largely, creates the time in which it happens."[3]

Although she claimed to be one of Hawthorne's descendants, O'Connor looked on place in a quite different way. Hawthorne accepts Salem, his "native place," because of its traditions which can be defined as "the habitual actions, habits, and customs . . . of the same people living in the same place."[4] However, Hawthorne was "invariably happiest elsewhere." Despite his need to anchor fiction in history and tradition, he gives his allegiance to a recollected image, not an actual place. In "The Custom House," he writes: "Soon, likewise, my own native town will loom upon me through the haze of memory, a mist brooding over and around it; as if it were no portion of the real earth, but an overgrown village in Cloud-land. . . . Henceforth, it ceases to be a reality in my life. I am a citizen of somewhere else." For O'Connor, nostalgia traps people in time and anchors them in place, connecting them with death instead of with the creating power of prospective metaphor. She uses speech rather than history to make her fiction appear au-

---

[3] George Steiner, *After Babel* (New York: Oxford University Press, 1981), p. 138.

[4] T. S. Eliot, quoted in Frank Kermode, *The Sense of an Ending* (New York: Oxford University Press, 1967), p. 112.

thentic. For her history possesses no value or value-making power, if viewed as a temporal series of events. History as metaphor, however, provides her with what Eliot called "The backward look behind the assurance / Of recorded history. . . ."

In only one story, "A Late Encounter With the Enemy," does O'Connor deal directly with history and historical place names. A middle-aged school teacher uses her old grandfather, who has fought in the Civil War, to add both dignity and authority to her delayed graduation from college. The old man, it turns out, is a bogus general who has exploited his reputation in order to gain respect and adulation. He has forgotten his past: "The past and the future were the same to him; one forgotten and the other not remembered." Moreover, the past is a dead language without living meaning, a collection of place names that no longer carry import or significance: ". . . the old words began to stir in his head as if they were trying to wrench themselves out of place and come to life." O'Connor's metaphor attempts to enliven the past, but like her "graduates in their black gowns," history collaborates with death, a "black procession." The old man's derangement increases until the climax of the story:

> . . . then a succession of places—Chickamauga, Shiloh, Marthasville—rushed at him as if the past were the only future now and he had to endure it. Then suddenly he saw that the black procession was almost on him. He recognized it, for it had been dogging all his days. He made such a desperate effort to see over it and find out what comes after the past that his hand clenched the sword until the blade touched bone.

His "vision" preceding his death seems a form without content; he has "forgotten the names of places and the places themselves," so that language no longer provides him vital consolation. Using a rare conceit, O'Connor shows how mere words divorced from the life they serve become spectres of our very being: "The words began to come toward him. . . . He couldn't protect himself from the words . . . like musket fire . . . a regular volley of them . . . he felt his body riddled. . . ." Ironically, the writer has used metaphor to evoke a world without metaphor, the dead letter of his history without a transfiguring vision, a supreme fiction. Metaphor is the poet's means of blocking the current running from past to future, denying causality, and rescuing man from the "black procession" of materialism.

O'Connor refuses to be trapped in historical time because history cannot make a life authentic. Tarwater in *The Violent Bear it Away*, having burned his country place, nevertheless returns from the city to reclaim his vision of it. He senses "a strangeness about the place," and his vision produces stasis, arrests physical or literal progress. Like Hazel Motes, "he appeared to be permanently suspended there unable to go forward or back." Recognizing that place is not landscape, he discovers his essential alienation: he will never find his place in the world. However, O'Connor provides him a way out, upward through metaphor:

He felt his hunger no longer as a pain but as a tide. He felt it *rising* in himself through time and darkness, *rising* through the centuries, and he knew that it *rose* in a line of men whose lives were chosen to sustain it, who would wander in the world, strangers from that violent country where the silence is never broken except to shout the truth. He felt it building from the blood of Abel to his own, *rising* and engulfing him. It seemed in one instant to *lift* and turn him. He whirled toward the treeline. There, *rising* and spreading in the night, a red-gold tree of fire *ascended* as if it would consume the darkness in one tremendous burst of flame [my emphasis].

He has been given companionable aliens, drawn not from history but from the myth that transforms Christian history into more than a "black procession."

Even while O'Connor estranges her characters from old and stable social contexts, she brings them to a new level of consciousness through metaphor. The earlier version of "The Displaced Person," published in the *Sewanee Review*, focuses on a farm woman, Mrs. Shortley. She and her husband are replaced on the farm by Mr. Guizac, a Polish refugee, and as a consequence Mrs. Shortley has a stroke and dies. The story charts her awakening consciousness, which causes her to become "displaced in the world from all that belonged to her." Mrs. Shortley is ignorant, fearful of change, intolerant—she remarks of the refugees, "They ain't where they belong to be at"—but when she becomes separated from her familiar surroundings, she turns to the Bible and through religious vision transcends her own unstable and vulnerable scene: "It was of no definite shape but there were fiery wheels with fierce dark eyes in them, spinning rapidly all around it. She was not able to tell if the figure was going forward or backward because its magnificence was so great. She shut her eyes. . . ." The vision from Ezekiel replaces her outer world so that when her eyes are later directed toward exterior place, "all the vision in them might have been turned around, looking inside her." Consequently, at her death, she approaches a transcendent vision, although from a worldly viewpoint she only *"seems* to contemplate for the first time the tremendous frontiers of her true country" [my emphasis]. Mrs. Shortley is left on the border of truth and the reader on the threshold of meaning.

When O'Connor revised the story for inclusion in *A Good Man is Hard to Find*, she added a further story, which explores the effect of the displaced person on Mrs. McIntyre, the owner of the farm. Like Mrs. Cope in "A Circle in the Fire," Mrs. McIntyre reiterates: "This is my place." Implicated in the death of the foreigner, she suffers unacknowledged guilt and remorse, until she becomes mentally rather than physically displaced: "she felt she was in some foreign country." Even before her involvement in Mr. Guizac's murder, however, Mrs. McIntyre suffers "interior violence" that will change her life. Prior to any physical action, she experiences its metaphoric equivalent: she "folded her arms as if she were equal to anything. But her heart was beating as if some interior violence had already been done to her." The "real" concluding experience of both women, Mrs. Shortley and Mrs. McIntyre, cannot be represented: one is in limbo and the other in purgatory, if we can employ these terms as metaphors and not as conceptual places.

Although O'Connor accurately observes how manners condition social behavior (and in her personal life adhered strictly to conventional social codes) her writing rejects class hierarchy, social decorum, the idea of keeping in one's place. Her characters are subordinated to action, and, as in poetry, action is finally subordinated to metaphor. The relation between the two parts of "The Displaced Person," each with its differing resolution, cannot be discovered by analyzing social relations. The reader must make his own resolution. As William Empson says of poetry:

two statements are made as if they were connected, and the reader is forced to consider their relationship for himself. The reason why these facts should have been selected for a poem is left for him to invent; he will invent a variety of reasons and order them in his own mind. This, I think, is the essential fact about the poetical use of language.[5]

And O'Connor said much the same thing, when she defended her literary practice:

We find that connections which we would expect in the customary kind of realism have been ignored, that there are strange skips and gaps which anyone trying to describe manners and customs would certainly not have left.

Thus "place," which would ordinarily represent a verifiable reality, becomes in O'Connor's hand a metaphoric means of apprehending what lies beyond her environment, not the thing seen, but a way of seeing.

The bumper sticker reads: "Smile: God loves You." And we recall the various photographs of Flannery O'Connor, looking dour, preoccupied, unwilling to be diluted by social amenities; caught in a snapshot, she sometimes looks like Sabbath Lily in *Wise Blood*, who "grinned suddenly and then drew her expression back altogether as if she smelled something bad." We further recall her gallery of unsmiling misfits, maintaining their integrity by refusing to share in society's power of positive thinking. Wary of smiles as an animal of a trap, O'Connor turns a commonplace gesture into

[5] William Empson, *Seven Types of Ambiguity* (New York: New Directions Books, 1953), p. 32.

a metaphor, constructing a generally consistent iconography, in which a smile stands for more than itself. Like a cliché, a smile can mask genuine private emotion; but like surface beauty, a smile can disguise fraudulent intentions that we believe in at our peril. Besides expressing a sense of well-being, smiles can reveal that we accept ourselves as well as others; and in agreeing to assume a social role, we deal with society on its own terms; a smiling response to a speaker generally may imply that one is a member of the speaker's circle. In all her fiction, O'Connor deals with characters who remain outside of any "circle," any community of shared responses. Their unsmiling faces indicate their rejection of role playing. On the other hand, the author also pictures the smiles of people willing to adjust to whatever role society assigns them. Mrs. Watts, the prostitute in *Wise Blood*, represents those happily at home in the world: "Mrs. Watts' grin was as curved and sharp as the blade of a sickle. It was plain that she was so well-adjusted that she didn't have to think anymore." A request to smile appears innocent enough: "It never hurt anyone to smile," says Mrs. Turpin in "Revelation"; and Mrs. Hopewell in "Good Country People" echoes the cliché, a "smile never hurt anyone." But for O'Connor, smiles can hurt profoundly, by encouraging social conformity that can lead to the death-in-life of empty rituals. In *Wise Blood*, the Devil is a pleasant friend, "grinning wisely."

A natural, undeceptive, and unselfconscious smile is rare in O'Connor's fiction, being reserved for very young children (the baby in "A Good Man is Hard to Find," the young boy in "The River," the black child in "Everything that Rises Must Converge," and the idiot Bishop in *The Violent Bear it Away*), for the innocent outsider entering society for the first time (the Polish immigrant in "The Displaced Person"), or for those adults who are natives yet not wholly of this world: the priest "smiling absently" or the mental patient "smiling toothlessly." Only after she has received her violent education from the Misfit does the grandmother in "A Good Man is Hard to Find" uncover a genuine smile: "With her legs crossed under her like a child's and her face smiling up at the cloudless sky." Although we accept smiling and laughing as inherent in the human species, we soon become aware that for O'Connor a smile is no natural expression but a figure of speech indicating a character's moral nature, a key to the hidden motives that govern action.

In "Everything That Rises Must Converge," O'Connor creates a situation in which social rituals, metaphorically represented by smiling, serve to bring about altered states of consciousness. The story belongs in the end to the young man Julian, who discovers the unsmiling nature of reality when his mother collapses, but the central plot concerns the encounter between his mother, a product of white supremacy, and a black woman whose smoldering resentment flares up in violence. In other O'Connor stories, smiles indicate that blacks accept stereotypical roles which demand gestures without genuine meaning—"The two of them came in grinning and shuffled to the side of the bed"—but in this anomalous story she questions whether facial expression can ever represent interior truth. By placing an angry Negro woman who rejects smiles of condescension next to Mrs. Chestney who grew up in an era when smiles promoted social harmony, though not racial equality, O'Connor approaches her true subject, which transcends topical issues.

Mrs. Chestney enters the bus as one enters one's *circle*, "with a little smile as if she were going into a drawing room where everyone has been waiting for her." Annoyed by his mother's ignorance of the current social situation, Julian takes a perverse pleasure in exposing what he sees as her hypocritical attitude toward black people. When his mother discovers that she and the black woman are wearing identical hats, Julian experiences satanic pleasure: "Justice entitled him to laugh. His grin hardened until it said to her as plainly as if he were saying it aloud: Your punishment exactly fits your pettiness." The justice without mercy behind Julian's grin contrasts with his mother's smiling at the Negro woman and her "grinning" child. But O'Connor in this story, advocates *neither* smile and, as usual in her stories, we need to be aware of who is interpreting facial or verbal expressions. Julian reports of his mother: "She kept her eyes on the woman and an amused smile came over her face *as if the woman were a monkey that had stolen her hat*" [my emphasis]. Julian interprets (reads his meaning into) his mother's smile and continues to explain her private emotions:

> "I think he likes me," Julian's mother said, and smiled at the woman.
>
> It was the smile she used when she was being particularly gracious to an inferior.

Not only does he know what lies behind his mother's expressions, he assumes a god-like knowledge of the mind and feelings of her black counterpart: "Julian could feel the rage in her at having no weapon like his mother's smile." O'Connor conveys the contempt (and cruelty) of Julian's smile, but his mother's condescension remains unproved, though perhaps real. However, even though Mrs. Chestney's consciousness may be corrupt, she does engage in human relations, whereas her son is like some Hawthorne character who discovers that seeing into the nature of sin is worse than sinning itself. O'Connor does not choose sides or express her personal views on racial integration; she is more concerned with the destructive power of selfishness and pride. She wrote to a friend: "The topical is poison. I got away with it in 'Everything That Rises' but only because I say a plague on everybody's house as far as the race business goes."

O'Connor's ironic detachment from social issues makes "Everything that Rises Must Converge" one of her finest stories, and her refusal to accept any smile at face value contributes to the story's unsettled meanings. However, in most of her other fiction, a smile is what Julian calls a "weapon," the community's means of promoting the status quo or its sign advertising the best of all possible worlds. Throughout her first novel, *Wise Blood*, the central character never smiles (he laughs once in disbelief), whereas most of the other characters join a smiling conspiracy that threatens his individuality, his relentless integrity. The false preacher Asa Hawks wears an expression "like a grinning mandrill" and his "edgy laugh" definitely associates him with the force of corruption. His smile is a mask concealing his true nature:

> "Look at this," Hawks said. He took a yellow newspaper clipping from his pocket and handed it to [Hazel Motes], and his mouth twisted out of the smile. "This is how I got the scars," he muttered. The child made a sign to him from the door to smile and not look sour. As he waited for Hazel to finish reading, the smile slowly returned.

The hypocrite preacher Onnie Jay Holy brings credit to his "Public Relations" profession: "He was not handsome but under his smile there was an honest look that fitted into his face like a set of false teeth." Even Enoch Emory, Hazel Motes's comic foil, owns an "evil crooked grin." Moreover, all of the women in the novel can be represented by Mrs. Leora Watts, or the bather with the "long and cadaverous" face: "She was facing them and she grinned. Enoch could see part of Hazel Motes's face watching the woman. It didn't grin in return. . . ." Somewhat later, the same face will appear "grinning on the glass, over Hazel Motes's." Since the devil is described as having a "grinning presence" it seems probable that in O'Connor's fiction a smile almost always brings one into collusion with the dishonest forces of the world. In her final novel, *The Violent Bear It Away*, the central character, like Hazel Motes, very rarely smiles as he moves through a world of smiling lawyers, salesmen, and his chief opponent, the schoolteacher Rayber, with a "smile of welcome and good will" that ironically indicates his association with the devil. When Tarwater does smile, he creates an instrument for unnerving Rayber, making Rayber question his own secret truth:

> The boy was looking directly at him with an omniscient smile, faint but decided. It was a smile that Rayber had seen on his face before. It seemed to mock him from an ever-deepening knowledge that grew in indifference as it came nearer and nearer to a secret truth about him.

Like the schoolteacher Rayber, Sheppard, the social worker in "The Lame Shall Enter First," uses smiling as a technique for bringing about social adjustment. O'Connor's aversion to sociology and psychology as cures for the ills of fallen man is pronounced: he "smiled to diminish the distance between them" and acknowledged that "half his effectiveness came from nothing more than smiling at them." Because social well-being does not represent spiritual well-being, O'Connor rejects both ethical and aesthetic cures for the human disease. The choice she presents to her characters (and hence to her readers) appears agonizing indeed: gain the world and lose your soul, or separate yourself from the world's unreliable appearances and become like the Old Testament prophets who never smile because they see through appearances to an end that is no laughing matter. No one *is* good even if he appears good (the lesson Mary Grace shocks Mrs. Turpin into learning in "Revelation") and Red Sammy, the "Fat Boy with the Happy Laugh" in "A Good Man is Hard to Find," can too soon become the "fat boy" with the "loose grin" who murders the vacationing family.

Despite her nearly schematic approach to the image of smiling, O'Connor remained quite aware that she was writing fiction and not engaging in polemics. She must show that there is a world between her two extreme positions. Metaphor must labor to ameliorate the agony and bring together two states or conditions. In "The River," the preacher "seemed almost but not quite to smile" (but finally doesn't); both Rufus Johnson and the Misfit "smiled slightly"; and Obadiah Elihue Parker, in "Parker's Back," sometimes wears an "uncertain grin." These equivocal gestures indicate O'Connor's difficulty in making a commitment to representation, the phenomenal base of metaphor. Only through symbol could she make image and ulterior meaning coalesce; by uniting smiles and frowns she would fuse comedy and tragedy into tragicomedy.

Probably O'Connor achieved her most remarkable integration of opposing forces in the icon of "The Artificial Nigger." Before they encounter this numinous figure, Mr. Head and Nelson commit the sin of pride, especially in regard to the Negro. Like those of other O'Connor characters, their smiles falsely elevate them above "inferiors," like the dining car waiter, just as smiles establish a bogus communion with their fellow white passengers. The black waiter has been put in his place by Mr. Head's wit and "all the travelers laughed and Mr. Head and Nelson walked out grinning." This triumph at another's expense is short-lived and ironically foreshadows their own "fall." (A similar pattern occurs in "Good Country People." Hulga maintains a glum face until she feels that she has gained control of the ignorant Bible salesman: "The girl smiled. It was the first time she had smiled at him at all." Almost immediately she is undone and her false redeemer, with the "pleasant laugh," in triumph abandons her.) Shortly, Mr. Head and Nelson are lost in the city, "wandering in a strange black place." Their sudden encounter with the plaster figure of a Negro brings together opposites, just as it "dissolves" their differences:

> It was not possible to tell if the artificial Negro were meant to be young or old; he looked too miserable to be either. He was meant to look happy because his mouth was stretched up at the corners but the chipped eye and the angle he was cocked at gave him a wild look of misery instead.

The smile merged with misery recalls the surrogate Jesus from *Wise Blood*: "His mouth had been knocked a little to one side so that there was just a trace of a grin covering his terrified look." Hazel Motes could not tolerate this corrupted image and threw it against the wall, but only a few years later, in "The Artificial Nigger," O'Connor created a similar image, only altering *the way it is seen*: "They stood gazing at the artificial Negro as if they were faced with some great mystery, some monument to another's victory that brought them together in their common defeat." To laugh at another is cruel, to laugh with another partakes of conformity, but to pay absolute attention, without judgment or explanation, is, as Simone Weil believed, a form of prayer. The wonder (or miracle) does not reside in the object but in the attention: to see *as if*, not simply to see.

A similar confrontation takes place in one of O'Connor's very last stories, "Judgement Day," a reworking of her first published story, "The Geranium," in which a white man, displaced in the North, finds his racial superiority undermined by the condescension of a black man who "had shiny tan shoes and was trying not to laugh and the whole business was laughing." In this later story, the white man's self-image has not only been thrown into doubt, it has also been redefined and ambiguously merged with that of the black man. As in "The Artificial Nigger," human pleasure and pain are one: the black man "looked directly at Tanner and grinned, or grimaced, Tanner could not tell which, but he had an instant's sensation of seeing before him a negative image of himself as if clownishness and captivity had been their common lot." Whether beautiful or ugly, social or antisocial, comic or tragic, the smile is a mask for a mystery that resists being divided into categories. But just as the self can bring about new forms of integration by dividing, so metaphor can lead to new definitions of the human condition. Only once in O'Connor's work do we find a genuine smile of unqualified joy, and it perhaps resembles the joy felt by the father when his prodigal son returns. In "The Enduring Chill," when the mother discovers that her "lazy ignorant conceited youth" will not die, but will be restored to health, she is overjoyed: "Her smile was as bright and intense as a light-bulb without a shade. 'I'm so relieved,' she said." However, this momentary, spontaneous overflow could not stand alone in any comprehensive representation of human experience, since it originates in pure pleasure, a release from the world's pain. Like Parker in "Parker's Back," O'Connor would not choose a "smiling Jesus" but instead a "flat stern Byzantine Christ with all-demanding eyes." If she were to recommend a smile to wear through the world, it would probably look like Tarwater's: "an odd smile, like some strange inverted sign of grief."

About a year before she died, O'Connor recalled a statue she saw at the Cloisters in New York: "It was the Virgin holding the Christ child and both were laughing; not smiling, laughing. I've never seen models of it anywhere but I was greatly taken with it and should I ever get back to the Cloisters, which is unlikely, I mean to see if it is there." How nicely is the fact of mortality ("which is unlikely") subordinated; and how fully she admires that exuberant laughter, unadulterated by the knowledge that soon it will subside into grief. However, her honesty as a writer of fictions demanded that she effect some metaphoric marriage of the pleasure and the pain she knew as "experience." Smiles were thus not the photographer's representative pleasure, clichés, but analogies of Being. O'Connor's repetitions of certain metaphors, smiles being but one, produce a pervasive iconography, again indicating that the writer's "method" depends less on plot, character, and verisimilitude than it does on a visionary poetics. The reader must question and continually reexamine gestures, both physical and verbal, in order to approach the hidden truth they so often misrepresent.

And then to play. The play's the thing. Play's
the thing. All virtue in "as if." "As if the last
days / Were fading and all wars were done."

As if they were. As if, as if!
— ROBERT FROST

As if—an ominous note. — NABOKOV

It was as if I were not a very ill old man; as if I
still had before me a whole lifetime; as if the
peace which possessed me were someone.
— MAURIAC

THE VIRTUE IN
AS IF

After Caroline Gordon read the manuscript of *The Violent
Bear it Away*, she suggested that O'Connor attend to certain verbal mannerisms, "technical imperfections" that had
become habitual. O'Connor was eager to comply, but she
wrote to a friend: "I have just corrected the page proofs and
I spent a lot of time getting *seems* and *as if* constructions out
of it. It was like getting ticks off a dog. I was blissfully unaware of all this while I was writing it. . . ." The stylistic tic
remained, however, despite the writer's conscious efforts,
and even in the typescript of a very late story, "Parker's
Back," we encounter numerous places where *as if* has been

cut or altered. O'Connor's problem persisted, perhaps because it was a symptom of some deeper struggle to work out her unconscious poetics. Editorial variants could hardly do more than disguise the difficulty the author was having in bringing about the marriage of fiction and belief, of worldly analogy and that mysterious power that undermines the ultimate value of the here and now.

Readers generally recognize the economy and compression of O'Connor's style, but the meaning hovering over her *as if* construction may need some exploration. The compound conjunction is composed of a direct comparison *as* followed by a conditional *if* that undermines the validity of the comparison. Thus *as if*, and variants like *as though*, function midway between a simile or analogy (i.e., something that she presents as objectively verifiable) and metaphor, poetic utterance that is concerned with how we see. (The construction also appears in Latin, *quasi*; French, *comme si*, *que si*; and German, *als ob*.)[1] For a writer striving to unite knowledge of her local region ("manners") with a singular vision ("mystery") the *as if* construction became the marriage ring. "The direction of many of us," she wrote, "will be more toward poetry than toward the traditional novel." Neither social realism on one hand nor Roman Catholic doctrine on the other can explain her characters' behavior. The words tell us to look for meaning between the *as* and the *if*, in what Coleridge called the poet's realm, the "intermundium" between the real and the imagined. And a striking piece of evidence that demonstrates the absurdity of a literal or "realistic" reading of O'Connor's fiction occurs at the end of "A View of the Woods." After killing his grand-

---

[1] Hans Vaihinger, *The Philosophy of "As If,"* trans. C. K. Ogden (New York: Barnes and Noble, Inc., 1952), p. 91. I have taken my description directly from Vaihinger, although I apply it to prose fiction in ways he never intended.

daughter, Mr. Fortune suffers a heart attack and realizes his need for "someone to help him." His heart expands so fast that he "felt *as if* he were being pulled after it through the woods, felt *as if* he were running. . . ." Desperately wanting a way out of his situation, he imagines an "opening":

It grew as [if] he ran toward it until suddenly the whole lake opened up before him. . . .

This typographical error, the omission of the essential "if" (which remains uncorrected), has caused some readers to picture the old man actually running, instead of imagining flight.

It should come as no surprise that O'Connor was drawn to the "romance" of Hawthorne, who reiterated that it was not his intention to "describe local manners." Both writers, however, needed to ground their fictions in the "as," Hawthorne in history and O'Connor in local idiom, before they could go about their business. We are aware in both writers, as in Conrad, of the pressure of the unknown upon the known, but in neither is the tension relieved by allowing the fiction to lose its fictionality, the *as if* to become a *because* or a *so that*. The pervasive presence of the *as if* in O'Connor's work belies the explanatory voice heard in her letters and occasional essays. Only when the writer overtly attempts to resolve fictional ambiguity (as we shall see later when we look at her difficulty with endings) does she weaken the literary form. When O'Connor maintains the *as if*, in spite of logical inconsistency—as Hazel Motes is a Christian *malgré lui*—the fiction retains its integrity.

The opening of almost any O'Connor narrative reveals the polarity, the known and unknown between which events oscillate. In *Wise Blood*: "Hazel Motes sat at a forward angle on the green plush train seat, looking one minute at the window *as if* he might want to jump out of it, and the next down the aisle at the other end of the car." (For emphasis, I shall italicize *as if* throughout.) The physical confinement he suffers signals that he needs to reorient his life, but his dilemma becomes a false one, that he can resolve only by immersing himself in the physical world or by taking himself out of it altogether. However, this either/or choice would destroy the productive tension between the literal and the metaphoric. Perhaps his situation also suggests O'Connor's early writing dilemma (likewise a false one): to write strictly regional fiction in the manner of Erskine Caldwell or to head North and escape the limitations inherent in the subject matter at hand. At the end of the novel when Hazel Motes rejects the world, blinds himself, and subsequently dies, he projects the author's coming into being, her refusal to "take what's offered you" ("place" as a limitation, and a given literary form called prose fiction) and her acceptance of the counter-factual realm of the poetic imagination. However, after Hazel Motes leaves the novel, the tension remains, and O'Connor transfers the *as if* construction to his surviving landlady, Mrs. Flood: "She felt *as if* she were blocked at the entrance of something. She sat staring with her eyes shut, into his eyes, and felt *as if* she had finally got to the beginning of something she couldn't begin. . . ." Mrs. Flood becomes the subject of another story of evolving consciousness.

In "The River," a later short story, O'Connor focuses the *as if* on young Harry Ashfield whose death by drowning has engendered considerable debate over whether a child of four or five can choose his salvation. Like Hazel Motes, the child faces a squalid existence, but unlike Motes he has no religious background against which he can define himself. Bound to an atheistic and materialistic family, he lacks the energy of conflict; he seems passive, almost an automaton, until he encounters the possibility of an escape from the known, and thereby a new identity. After his babysitter introduces him to the story of Christ in a book, his mind becomes dislocated; "dreamy and serene," he recognizes the world as an incomplete place. The author endows him with metaphoric energy: "*as if* he wanted to dash off and snatch the sun." That same sun, a little before, had also begun to emerge from its material condition, to seek something beyond itself: "The white Sunday sun followed at a little distance, climbing fast through a scum of gray cloud *as if* it meant to overtake them." Dynamic power in O'Connor, so often expressed through violent metaphors, can transform people and the natural world, but she refuses to declare the transformation except by the ambiguous means of *as if*. Only within the poet's vision can the world become more than itself: "he had never been in the woods before and he walked carefully, looking from side to side *as if* he were entering a strange country." If now we see through a glass darkly, the fiction writer's *as if* does little to reduce that obscurity. O'Connor's writing does not represent the physical world but serves as her means of apprehending and understanding a power activating that world. Thus she is true to Coleridge's (and essentially Aristotle's) idea of mimesis: she does not copy external form; she imitates the life that animates both man and nature. The *as if* is her bridge between the real and the imagined, but it is a bridge that cannot carry her or us to the other side.

Only in the Christian paradox, declaimed in "The River" by the fundamentalist preacher at the river baptism, does the *as if* disappear. Truth replaces fiction, as the language turns duality into identity. The "old water river," as the preacher calls it, becomes more than itself. It is variously the river of life, the river of blood, the river of faith, the river of love, the river of pain, and the river of suffering. The "of" certainly does not function like *as if* to alert us to possible fictionality. There is only *one* river, says the preacher, and "*if* you believe, you can lay your pain in *that* River" [my emphasis]. When the child returns later to baptize himself, he has come to believe that the Kingdom of Christ is *in* the river. The incarnation has become a reality to him; what he imagined has become a mortal fact.

After Harry Ashfield (with his new identity as Bevel) returns home from the river, the ugliness of his surroundings intensifies, and the *as if* construction disappears from the story, except for two key passages dealing exclusively with the boy. Separated from the transcendent vision that redefined and elevated him, he can recreate it in time and space only by means of his imagination. Things held in faith cannot, according to Aquinas, be both seen and believed at the same time—even Thomas "*saw one thing and believed another*," i.e., saw man but through faith also saw God.[2] In the preacher's speech and in the boy's consciousness two realms may interpenetrate, but like the terms of metaphor they remain separable in the reader's mind. The child imagines the reality of his mother away:

> He shut his eye and heard her voice from a long way away, *as if* he were under the river and she on top of it. She shook his shoulder. "Harry," she said, leaning down and putting her mouth to his ear, "tell me what the preacher said." She pulled him into a sitting position and he felt *as if* he had been drawn from under the river.

[2] St. Thomas Aquinas, *Summa Theologica* (New York: Benzinger Brothers, Inc., 1947), "On Faith," Article IV, p. 1171.

Between two stages of being, he clearly rejects the corrupt material world and desires to be under the river, but the writer can point only toward a *possible* transformation: "Very slowly, his expression changed *as if* he were gradually seeing appear what he didn't know he was looking for. Then all of a sudden he knew what he wanted to do." Between the appearance and his impulsive knowledge, an action occurs that remains inexplicable. Although the child seeks his meaning in the river—not *as if* it were there—we as spectators witness an ambiguous resolution. After a struggle, the river takes him, and "since he was moving quickly and knew he was getting somewhere, all his fury and fear left him." His "somewhere" may be in or out of space. Whether little Harry Ashfield is saved or not remains a consideration irrelevant to the experience of the story. Like Hazel Motes, the boy has closed his eyes to earthly resemblance and the man who attempts to "save" him (ironically called Mr. Paradise) is yoked to the physical, and resembles "a giant pig." O'Connor's "The River," like most of her stories, dictates no single overt meaning but an interaction of meanings: the *as* of direct analogy with the indefinite, conditional *if*.

Despite O'Connor's desire to see and believe at the same time, the recurring *as if* in her stories denies any merger of the dual entities that constitute metaphor. She can write to a friend: "I believe the Host is actually the body and blood of Christ, not a symbol." And, she recalls, several years earlier, making the startling remark concerning the Eucharist, "If it's a symbol, to hell with it," but in her work, she constantly struggles against identity. Apparently conceiving of "symbol" as mere "sign," she perhaps had not encountered Coleridge's more "incarnating" definition of symbol as that which "partakes of the reality it renders intelligible" or that which "enunciates the whole" and yet "abides itself as a living part of that unity of which it is the representative."³ (She appeared to enlarge her definition later, however, when she referred to a "living symbol.") In practice, O'Connor avoided merging the two parts of her metaphor, even at epiphanic moments. For example, in "The Artificial Nigger": "They stood gazing at the artificial Negro *as if* they were faced with some great mystery. . . ." O'Connor's God is not truly the "father" of men, but treated *as if* he were, and to deny the identity of bread and body, wine and blood does not undermine spiritual efficacy but asserts the supreme fiction that transcends the limits of representational language and unites us in a creating process. Northrop Frye's comment could apply to our real or fictional experience: "Whether we think it *is* true or not matters little, in actual life: there, it is the determination to make it true, to live as though [*as if*] individual and class were an identity, that is important."⁴ Certainly O'Connor in theory or fiction would have avoided the heresy of identifying God with his creation.

The struggle that both Hazel Motes and Harry Ashfield undergo in trying to resolve the tension between the *as* and the *as if* might appear characteristic of any fiction writer who must somehow convert utilitarian language into a means of revelation. Both empirical fact and the literal word must be renovated, as both Hawthorne and O'Connor demonstrate. However, a brief glance at another writer who meant much to O'Connor shows that this is not always so. In Poe, a pattern of direct relation more often dominates: "as I fled," "as I placed," "as I felt," "as he whispered," "as it

³ Coleridge's well-known definition of symbol appears in *The Stateman's Manual*. Samuel Taylor Coleridge, *Lay Sermons*, ed. R. J. White (Princeton: Princeton University Press, 1972), p. 30.
⁴ Northrop Frye, *The Great Code: The Bible and Literature* (New York: Harcourt, Brace, Jovanovich, 1982), p. 228.

came." Because Poe is a writer who aspires to an imaginative realm uncorrupted by fact, the *as if* construction rarely occurs. Capable of severing his connection to time and space, Poe spends no time constructing those bridges that both Hawthorne and O'Connor rely on. More confident of the supremacy of fiction, Poe allows it to pursue its unimpeded life, and he has little need for language as an instrument for understanding the world. Thus in "The Fall of the House of Usher" only a few *as ifs* appear and they mostly serve to convey subordinated information that little affects Poe's direct evocation of scene and character. In general, the *as* component of the *as if* is more appropriate because things appear to Poe with no need for linguistic evasion. They do not *seem* to appear:

> I did actually hear (although from what direction it proceeded I found it impossible to say) a low and apparently distant, but harsh, protracted, and most unusual screaming or grating sound—the exact counterpart of what my fancy had already conjured up for the dragon's unnatural shriek as described by the romancer.

Although some ambiguity exists as to whether the sound is a screaming or a grating, there is no uncertainty that the sound is heard or that it reproduces the imaginary one. Unlike O'Connor's fiction, which uses metaphor to assure a disparity between the given world and how we view it, Poe's fiction presents itself as real and, like a dogma, cannot be questioned. However, it has subjective validity only, and language need not labor to find an end when it is an end in itself. The narrator of "Berenice" could speak for Poe: "The realities of the world affected me as visions, and as visions only, while the wild ideas of the land of dreams became, in turn, not the material of my everyday existence, but in very deed that existence utterly and solely in itself."

The *as if* does not tolerate any reading of experience as unambiguous, "utterly and solely in itself." Interpreters (including O'Connor herself when she retrospectively interpreted her own words) tend to fashion a way out of the difficulties often arising at the climaxes of stories, those places where what she called mystery and manners meet. In "A Good Man is Hard to Find," O'Connor prevents the reader, in his insatiable need to explain behavior, from intruding on the privacy of her characters' minds. The story, what she called her "little romance," begins in satire and ends, for some, in tragedy, but it is certainly not "realistic." If the writer had chosen either to remain exclusively outside her characters (as with the wife, her face "as broad and innocent as a cabbage") or to provide us with an account of the workings of their minds, she might have produced in either case a consistently satisfying story. But the *as if* blocks us from agreeable meaning; in effect, we are always unsatisfied, on the threshold of meaning. When the grandmother recognizes the Misfit, he smiles slightly *"as if* he were pleased in spite of himself to be known." Each subsequent description follows a formula: a declarative gesture, followed by an evasive statement of what hides behind gesture (the first example containing a double evasion, *seemed* and *as if*):

He seemed to be embarrassed *as if* he couldn't think of anything to say. . . .

The Misfit said . . . *as if* he had considered her statement carefully. . . .

The Misfit looked . . . *as if* he were embarrassed again. . . .

The Misfit said *as if* he agreed. . . .

Needless to say, the author's *as if* denies the reader any direct entrance into the Misfit's thought and offers no unequivocal means of comprehending his behavior—we must supply our own motive. We are thus implicated in his disturbing experience. The absence of direct statement may further indicate that the author is reluctant to appropriate a truly omniscient role: to know the secret of character, the secret of natural happening, the secrets of the words themselves. Regardless of her strategy, the climax of "A Good Man is Hard to Find" contains gestures whose meaning has not been clearly articulated:

She saw the man's face twisted close to her own *as if* he were going to cry and she murmured, "Why you're one of my babies. You're one of my children." The Misfit sprang back *as if* a snake had bitten him and shot her three times in the chest.

In a discarded fragment, describing the scene after the accident, O'Connor wrote: " 'Count the children, count the children!' Granny screamed, for her thoughts were always for others." But this characterizing insight does not appear in the published story, so that we are left with a woman of words, *shown* to be devious, self-satisfied, clothed in superficial manners. In contrast, the Misfit, aware of his spiritual inadequacy, strives to be honest, visibly struggles to know himself. The story does not direct us to choose sides in this engagement of opposing forces, as commentators are sometimes prone to do. Even O'Connor's own explanation of the ending falters. Leaving the fictional mode for the mode of critical analysis, she turns her *as if* into an *as*: "The Misfit is touched by the Grace that comes through the old lady when she recognizes him as her child, as she has been touched by the Grace that comes through him in his particular suffering." We could well argue, from the text, that O'Connor has happily failed to demonstrate the clear resolution her commentary provides. The grandmother's evident sentimentality (her distortion or evasion of reality) could be found in her cry, "Why you're one of my babies." The Misfit's violence ("*as if* a snake had bitten him") would consequently be a reaction to the serpent's tongue. To approach the unknown, the story may be saying, one must first comprehend the inadequacy of the known, and the Misfit is correct when he declares that Christ has "thrown everything off balance." Unlike the balanced comparisons of *like* and *as*, built on similarity, O'Connor's *as if* also throws everything off balance. The story lingers in the mind, precisely because of the uncertainty of meaning behind her characters' gestures and words. To diminish the story's potentialities sometimes appears to be the job of clarifying critics. But readers of fiction will continue to distinguish, in the words of Robert Graves, "The thundering text, the snivelling commentary."[5]

The complex meanings evoked by O'Connor's *as if* center on power, an inexplicable energy acting on the mind and on or through external nature. This power cannot be named; language can only render its effects. If we see metaphor as "saying one thing while meaning another," we can understand why customary metaphor proved inadequate to O'Connor's special needs. Seeking to incorporate power, she required not a condensed simile, confining her to the phenomenal world, but a comparison lying somewhere between a true resemblance and an actual equivalence. What follows the *as if* does not explain what precedes it. What the

[5] Robert Graves, "Ogres and Pygmies," *Collected Poems* (New York: Anchor Books, 1966), p. 106.

Misfit says or does is not clarified, but obscured, by analogy: "The Misfit sprang back *as if* a snake had bitten him." Because the action is described but not evaluated, because motive remains hidden behind impulse, we find that some violence has been done to cause-and-effect experience— and to what we can expect from language. We could speculate that it is not images of physical violence in O'Connor's work that unsettles so many readers—current novels, films, or television programs contain far more—but the violence done to familiar ways of thinking: the good man is hard to find because he cannot be defined. "The dictionary contains no metaphors," says Paul Ricoeur,[6] and only through metaphor can O'Connor point toward the good that is always "something under construction," the "process" of understanding.

The realistic guise under which most of O'Connor's stories begin is discarded as they progress, and in her design on the reader she resembles Chekhov: "I conduct the entire action peacefully and quietly," Chekhov wrote, "but at the end I punch the reader in the nose." Both, however, seek not to exploit sensation but rather to alter consciousness. In O'Connor's case, the violent power associated with the unknown is evoked by the complement of *as if*. Integral to the fabric of the writing, it takes form as event or action only as a means of temporarily resolving the story. In her fiction, the significance of a violent physical act can be discovered only in the verbal acts preceding it.

O'Connor had the ending of "Greenleaf" in mind before she started writing the story, but she was unaware of how the event would take on meaning: "I plan for the heroine, aged 63, to be gored by a bull. I am not convinced yet that

---

[6] Paul Ricoeur, *The Rule of Metaphor* (Toronto: University of Toronto Press, 1977), p. 97.

this is a purgation or whether I identify myself with her or the bull." However, she acknowledges in her opening line the violent force that acts through man and external nature: "Mrs. May's bedroom window was low and faced on the east and the bull, silvered in the moonlight, stood under it, his head raised *as if* he listened—like some patient god come down to woo her—for a stir inside the room." But only the animal's head, decorated by simile, is a "fact"; everything that follows the *as if* qualifies as figure, the simile only extending the unreality. As the story progresses, each complement of the *as if* intensifies the power of the unnamable force for which the bull is only a synecdoche. Mrs. May hears a "rhythmic chewing *as if* something were eating one wall"—a *something* that appears in many stories, in contrast to the *nothing* that names life without a transfiguring vision. That force assumes a metaphoric form other than the bull when Mrs. May comes upon Mrs. Greenleaf in the throes of a religious seizure: "Mrs. May stopped still, one hand lifted to her throat. The sound was so piercing that she felt *as if* some violent unleashed force had broken out of the ground and was charging toward her." As we shall see later, when we look at "Greenleaf" in more detail, the force includes the unfocused fears that drive Mrs. May, as well as O'Connor's other matriarchs. After confronting her son's "furious charge of energy," Mrs. May subsides into a customary discourse and decorum: "all her resources returned to full strength *as if* she had only to be challenged by the devil himself to regain them." Like the grandmother's in "A Good Man is Hard to Find," however, Mrs. May's resources prove useless in the end: calling the Misfit "good" is as absurd as calling the "violent and unleashed force" the devil. Samuel Johnson complained that with the metaphysical poets "heterogenous ideas are yoked by violence together" and he further could not accept the possibility that language could deal with good and evil as forces: "The good and evil of eternity are too ponderous for the wings of wit; the mind sinks under them, in passive helplessness, content with calm belief and humble adoration."[7] But O'Connor, by means of her *as if*, unleashes the power that shatters decorum, agitates "calm belief." Like Blake, she realizes that "none by traveling over known lands can find out the unknown."[8] At the end of the story, "something" emerges and becomes embodied in the bull, "*as if* he were overjoyed to find her again." In "freezing unbelief," she "stared at the violent black streak bounding toward her, *as if* she had no sense of distance, *as if* she could not decide at once what his intention was. . . ." After being gored, she is described indirectly; she looks *as if* she has received illumination: "She had the look of a person whose sight had been suddenly restored but who finds the light unbearable." It is not the bull but the light (the knowledge) that is unbearable; the bull emerges as a violent lover who saves her from unconsciousness. Violence may proceed from love, or hate, but hardly from indifference.

In the human imagination good consorts with evil, opposites partake of each other, and this is why, half-humorously, O'Connor referred to her "evil imagination." Of American writers, she seems closest to Hawthorne, particularly in her fascination with those people who proceed beyond the boundaries of conventional "good behavior." In both, however, the language of fiction complicates rather than simplifies the "moral mission." Like Young Goodman Brown, O'Connor has been found so obsessively aware of

[7] Samuel Johnson, *Lives of the Poets*, "Milton" (New York: Doubleday and Co., n.d.), vol. 1, p. 137.

[8] William Blake, "All Religions are One," *The Complete Poetry and Prose of William Blake*, ed. David V. Erdman (New York: Anchor Books, 1982), p. 1.

sin that she cannot look on surface beauty or social harmony without finding hidden corruption. Although both writers accept a flawed humanity, O'Connor uses Hawthorne's "moonlight of romance" for an opposite effect in "The Artificial Nigger."

Hawthorne, less confident in his imagination, exclaims: "Blessed are all simple emotions, be they dark or bright! It is the lurid intermixture of the two that produces the illuminating blaze of the infernal regions."[9] The result of the imaginary journey recorded in "The Artificial Nigger" contrasts starkly with that of "Young Goodman Brown." Despite Hawthorne's yearning to resolve his ambiguities, his fictional impulse cannot be brought under control and converted into "simple emotions." Like the Minister's "black veil" or the "birthmark," forms of the *as if* (*seems, as though, as it were*) can be removed only by killing the fiction. For Hawthorne, the imagination presents alternate versions of "reality," and consciousness of both versions leads to despair or death. O'Connor's *as if* allows her to extend her unifying vision. And unlike Hawthorne, her method furthers a linguistic not a social engagement. Whereas Goodman Brown leaves his home and community and journeys into the wilderness in order to solve the mystery of evil, O'Connor's Mr. Head and Nelson leave nature behind in order to find their mystery within the community. In both stories, dislocation leads to a revelation of the dark forces within man and to an altered vision of the world; however, Goodman Brown's recognition of evil produces alienation from external nature *and* man, whereas in O'Con-

[9] Nathaniel Hawthorne, "Rappaccini's Daughter," *Mosses from an Old Manse* (New York: The Library of America, 1982), p. 987.

nor's story confrontation with sin and mystery leads to a "dissolving of differences" and a restoration to the natural world, which was created, and remains, unambiguously good.

The opening of "The Artificial Nigger" resonates with the ambiguity of appearance so familiar in Hawthorne:

> Mr. Head awakened to discover that the room was full of moonlight. He sat up and stared at the floor boards—the color of silver—and then at the ticking on his pillow, which might have been brocade, and after a second, he saw half of the moon five feet away in his shaving mirror, paused *as if* it were waiting for permission to enter.

The scene brings to mind "The Custom-House": "Thus, therefore, the floor of the familiar room has become neutral territory, somewhere between the real world and fairyland, where the actual and the imaginary meet, and each imbues itself with the nature of the other." O'Connor's story completes itself by returning to this "miraculous moonlight," but in between a drama occurs in which Mr. Head and Nelson confront the force of the unknown (in their limited vision represented by the Negro), just as Goodman Brown finds in the "devilish Indian" in the wilderness a threat to his mental security, his at-home consciousness. Hawthorne from the beginning undermines the veracity of Goodman Brown's journey, emphasizing "dream" and even "optical deception." Since Hawthorne is concerned with the interior nature of sin and less with its outward manifestation—"the fiend in his own shape is less hideous than when he rages in the heart of man"—Goodman Brown is brought from illusion to delusion. The *as if* dominates his outlook and his imagination becomes an alienating power: "He shrank from the venerable saint [and accepted truth?] *as if* to avoid an anathema," and he "snatched away the child *as if* from the grasp of the fiend himself." Hawthorne may only *question* the appearances of his fiction but he *demonstrates* its disastrous effect. Regardless of the "reality" of Goodman Brown's vision, it has produced authentic despair. Neither in "The Artificial Nigger" nor in other stories involving anguish and death does O'Connor doubt the redemptive power evoked by means of her visionary poetics.

Mr. Head, in O'Connor's story, takes his grandson into the city to introduce him to experience, to the facts of life, one fact being what a Negro is. (Since the boy has never seen one, a Negro can serve as the author's synecdoche for the unknown; however, mystery remains even after one has encountered *appearing* nature.) From the beginning, O'Connor's "mysterious moonlight" embraces both teacher and pupil, and indicates that all distinctions, like all definitions and all facts, are unsatisfying because incomplete, an *as* without an *if*: "Under the useless morning moon the tracks looked white and fragile. Both the old man and the child stared ahead *as if* they were waiting for an apparition." The story evidences the demand of the *as if* that one become lost to the ways of the world, to familiar resemblance: "He felt *as if* he were reeling down through a pitch-black tunnel." Dislocated, young Nelson wants to return home, to the familiar. In his reverie he encounters "black forms moving up from some part of him into the light," and these dynamic forms invigorate a world without metaphor: "The sun shed a dull dry light on the narrow street; everything looked like exactly what it was." The self-reflexive simile binds us to things *as they are*, the dead end of materialism, the impoverished fact. And again we recall Hawthorne (in "My Kinsman, Major Molineux"): "the moon, creating, like the imaginative power, a beautiful strangeness to familiar objects, gave something of romance to a scene that might not have possessed it in the light of day."

The violence that Nelson confronts is not external but arises solely as "black forms" from the unconscious that have assumed the threatening power of the Maenads: "The women were milling around Nelson *as if* they might suddenly all dive on him at once and tear him to pieces." Vulnerable, the boy turns to his "guide," Mr. Head, the superficial knowledge by which we try to make sense of the world. Ironically, Mr. Head himself is now "wandering into a black strange place," which is no place at all. The two, united in their common alienation and defeat, reach their nadir, the "heat without light" of the traditional Christian "hell."

As in other O'Connor narratives, sudden disclosure occurs, fortuitous in terms of plot or character, but prepared for by recurring metaphor: the presence of the unknown, summoned by means of the *as if*. The "plaster figure of a Negro" possesses no meaning except what is conferred on it by the imagination. Like the "narrow street," the Artificial Nigger is only a *thing* until the poet transforms it into a symbol that lies midway between the literal and the metaphorical.[10] The roles of the old man and the young child, a prideful reason and a prideful innocence, merge in the Negro statue: "It was not possible to tell if the artificial Negro were meant to be young or old; he looked too miserable to be either."

O'Connor tells us that the story originated in an over-

---

[10] Hawthorne and O'Connor both inhabit Coleridge's "intermundium," where fact and fiction mingle. Coleridge alerts readers to the limitations of categorical choice: "for such men it is either literal or metaphorical. There is no third. For to the Symbolical they have not arrived," *Collected Letters of Samuel Taylor Coleridge*, ed. E. L. Griggs (Oxford: Oxford University Press, 1956-1971), vol. V, 91.

heard *phrase*, in astonishing words, not in actual or conceptual experience. Words lingered in the mind until they could find embodiment in image and discover their life in symbol. The author exposes the misery of the human condition that the two characters are vaguely realizing. In her characteristic manner, she does not impose meaning on her characters' experience but simply describes its urgency.

> Mr. Head looked like an ancient child and Nelson like a miniature old man. They stood gazing at the artificial Negro *as if* they were faced with some great mystery, some monument to another's victory that brought them together in their common defeat. They could both *feel* it dissolving their differences like an action of mercy. . . . Nelson's eyes *seemed* to implore him to explain once and for all the mystery of existence [my emphasis].

Both Mr. Head and Nelson had earlier *seen* Negroes "going about their business *as if* they had been white," but now they *feel* a common humanity, a sense of communion that words can only suggest. The author does not intrude on "mystery"; the illumination need not be explained or questioned, only accepted for its awesome power. No *as if* need qualify the analogy of being. The train arrives at the station

> . . . just as the moon, restored to its full splendor, sprang from a cloud and flooded the clearing with light. As they stepped off, the sage grass was shivering gently in shades of silver and the clinkers under their feet glittered with a fresh black light. The treetops, fencing the junction, like the protecting walls of a garden, were darker than the sky which was hung with gigantic white clouds illuminated like lanterns.

Flannery O'Connor 70

The fiction can subside; nature is now suffused with the power that was once remote but is now quickening and freshening it. They have returned to Eden, reclaimed the innocence that they lost temporarily through selfishness and pride. Hawthorne's alienating vision allows no renovated Eden. Goodman Brown's fall seems to affect nature itself: "*as if* the roaring wind, the rushing streams, the howling beasts, and every other voice of the unconcerted wilderness were mingling and according with the voice of guilty man. . . ." Goodman Brown returns to a community that no longer exists for him. Metaphor summons alienation, not restoration.

In contrast to Hawthorne, O'Connor appears unconcerned with the relationship of the individual to an existing society; indeed, she consistently avoids depicting group activity, perhaps on the assumption that groups impede rather than further individual spiritual development. Mr. Head and Nelson are apparently changed, but the storyteller provides no indication that they will become good neighbors. Community for Hawthorne is an inescapable reality, confirmed by history; it can be questioned or even condemned but finally has to be accepted as our only means of finding personal fulfillment. By isolating oneself from the group, as does Goodman Brown, one loses oneself. For O'Connor, community is a metaphor, an *as if* having no temporal configuration. From her earliest work to her latest, we look in vain for scenes in which people function collectively. Hazel Motes's experience in the army, fairly extensive in manuscript, appears in *Wise Blood* as two slim paragraphs. And in what is probably her last story, "Parker's Back," the chief character is given no convincing social identity. The pool-hall scene in which he meets his "friends" is undeveloped and ends when he is thrown out: "then a calm descended on the pool hall as nerve-shattering *as if* the long barnlike room were a ship from which Jonah had been cast into the sea." O'Connor's characters do not inhabit neighborhoods, nor do they entertain friends, except by necessity. "They were not actually friends," she says in *Wise Blood*, "but he had to live with them." Alone, her characters await the arrival of apocalypse.

By isolating himself from his community, Goodman Brown allies himself with the forces of darkness, the devil who promotes individuality and a free imagination. But like Hester Prynne he has to remain within the community in order for "salvation" to be possible. Although O'Connor reiterated that the artist must keep "talking inside a community" and that "the knowledge that the novelist finds" must be found "in his community," she seems to have transferred to external nature the sacramental quality Hawthorne assigned to community. Goodman Brown discovers that nature possesses a negative power and he hears a chorus "not of human voices but of all the sounds of the benighted wilderness." Here nature houses the demonic, as in *The Scarlet Letter*: "Such was the sympathy of nature—that wild, heathen Nature of the forest, never subjugated by human law, nor illuminated by higher truth—with the bliss of these two spirits!" As "The Artificial Nigger" and her other fiction show, O'Connor redefines community as visionary and absolute. Unlike Hawthorne's historical conception of community, generation linked to generation through time, O'Connor's community is apocalyptic, so that finally communal and public acts, like real analogies, are incapable of representing interior value. The ultimate evocation of community in O'Connor occurs in "Revelation," when "a visionary light" reveals a "bridge extending upward from the earth through a field of living fire." (Christ the bridge-maker, the *pontifex*, assures the condition that fiction can only point toward). Hawthorne's ulterior dream was of a society that could embrace people's differences; O'Connor spoke of her "true country" where differences will be burned away (as in "Revelation") or dissolved (as in "The Artificial Nigger").

Until there is a single version of "reality," every writer of fiction lives *as if*, on the border between lives. It is not the "matter" that defines art but what one does with the matter. One cannot "really live" in O'Connor's "true country," but one can imagine it by the untruth of the *as if*.

SEEING INTO

MYSTERY

O'Connor's metaphors, particularly her characteristic *as if*, release a power, often violent and threatening, that demands the death of the understanding before the reader can begin to evolve a new consciousness. The power exists in man and in external nature, but it remains hidden to those who see *as* and not *as if*. Onnie Jay Holy, in *Wise Blood*, could represent all those literalists who cling to the assurance of the understanding: "You don't have to believe nothing you don't understand and approve of. If you don't understand it, it ain't true, and that's all there is to it. No jokers in the deck, friends." The power that O'Connor summons up by means of *as if* she calls a "presence"; however, the artist's task is not to name it but to activate it. Throughout her writing, the appearance of *as if* announces the arrival of a condition contrary to fact that we may call mystery. Her characters often exist in a kind of limbo, *feeling* what they cannot fully understand: one character changes his expression "*as if* he were gradually seeing appear what he didn't know he'd been looking for"; another feels "*as if* he were in the presence of a new personality"; another looks "*as if* he beheld some terrible compelling vision." And the characters in "The Artificial Nigger" enjoy no beatific vision: they gaze "*as if* they were faced with some great mystery." Thus metaphor makes it possible for a poet to engage a mystery she cannot define.

In her relentless need to discover fresh metaphors to act as "evidence of things not seen," O'Connor joins the company of other writers, and ones who do not share her religious orthodoxy. She was capable of maintaining a distinction between "defined mysteries" and the mystery that inhabits the natural world and works of art. She refers to "the mystery that James foresaw the loss of," and she even appropriated his phrase "mystery and manners" as a way of describing the subject matter of fiction. She further acknowledged her kinship with Hawthorne and Conrad, whose mysteries seem remote from the sacramental. Just as these "obscure" writers refuse to anchor mystery within the conceptual realm, we should be wary of importing a definition from outside O'Connor's fiction (whether from doctrine or dictionary). To define mystery not only limits its power but also its very mysteriousness. A word divorced from its context surrenders its life, and consequently its usefulness. "I shall not define the term," said Valéry of the term Romantic. "To attempt to do so would mean dispensing with all sense of precision."[1] In her very last story, "Parker's Back," we find O'Connor still struggling to find a form for mystery. The story has been said to illustrate a Roman Catholic heresy which claims that God did not possess a physical being, but this "idea" seems subordinate to the writer's more practical and immediate need: to find language that can deal with mystery without degrading it into concrete pictures.

In "Parker's Back," O'Connor creates an inarticulate and only dimly conscious protagonist as if initially doubting the power of rational discourse to engage mystery. Like Hazel Motes, O. E. Parker has been running from the unknown since his mother tried to save his soul. However, his first encounter with mysterious power takes place not in a church but at a fair where he is awakened to wonder by a tattooed man—not by the man himself but by an energy acting through him, an "arabesque of men and beasts and flowers on his skin" that "appeared to have a subtle motion of its own." Parker's subliminal experience changes him, but the change cannot be shown except by a metaphor that, paradoxically, denies him eyesight:

> Until he saw the man at the fair, it did not enter his head that there was anything out of the ordinary about the fact that he existed. Even then it did not enter his head, but a peculiar unease settled in him. It was *as if* a blind boy had been turned so gently in a different direction that he did not know his destination had been changed.

The *as if* awakens a paradox, and just as the passive blind boy is turned by an outside power so the reader is turned away from the representative function of language. He must

[1] Paul Valéry, *Leonardo, Poe, Mallarmé*, trans. Malcolm Cowley and James R. Lawler (Princeton: Princeton University Press, 1972), p. 196.

enter an interpretive process, moving toward an indeterminate end. Parker's "unease" progressively worsens, compelling him to get more and more tattoos; he hopes to allay by images the restless mystery. He tries to escape from himself, but even in the Navy he carries with him what O'Connor in another story calls "some interior violence." The mystery seems both exterior and interior: his eyes "reflect the immense spaces around him *as if* they were a microcosm of the mysterious sea." His incessant need for tattoos implies a life without ultimate meaning since each act provides only isolated, momentary satisfaction. His impulses are seeking a motive, but like language without a controlling method, he moves without direction. Each step seems a "leap forward into a worse unknown" until what begins as vague discontent ends as paranoia: "once or twice he found himself turning around abruptly *as if* someone were trailing him." This pursuing power, sometimes called a "presence," occurs often in O'Connor's work; for example, it threatens the young boy Powell in "A Circle in the Fire" ("*as if* something were after him") and even the sun appears to the young boy in "The River": "*as if* it meant to overtake him."

After he leaves the Navy, Parker marries ugly Sarah Ruth Cates, an act as inexplicable as his purchase of more tattoos. She may resemble that fundamentalist mother whom both he and Hazel Motes try to run away from, but, whatever her role, O'Connor provides her with no sympathetic traits. She is dour, unrelieved, even by O'Connor's customary humor. Her denial of the Church as an institution (and her Protestant distrust of icons) extends to the image of Christ that Parker, in the hope of pleasing her, eventually has tattooed on his back. To Sarah Ruth, all images, representations drawn from nature, are idolatrous. Because for her only *names* are worthy of reverence, she denies that the natural world can possibly provide any visual form for mystery. In courting her, Parker had kept his given names a secret while proudly displaying his body, covered with graven images. After swearing on "God's holy word" that she will not disclose his secret identity, Sarah Ruth experiences her own awe before mystery:

> "Obadiah," she whispered. Her face slowly brightened *as if* the name came as a sign to her. "Obadiah," she said. The name still stank in Parker's estimation. "Obadiah Elihue," she said in a reverent voice.

Clearly for Sarah Ruth words contain mystery, and, as she is incapable of comprehending an incarnational art, her repeated words suggest the power of incantation. O'Connor has thus presented a polarity: Parker would keep his name secret, but reveal his body; Sarah Ruth refuses the body (she will sleep with him only in total darkness) but insists that his name be spoken. By denying the physical world, Sarah Ruth rejects the ground for metaphor, and she shares this viewpoint with other O'Connor characters who suffer an impaired vision, such as Hulga in "Good Country People," who has "seen through to nothing" and "seldom paid any close attention to her surroundings." According to the "Analogy of Being,"[2] man can know God only by means of an intervening object: we love Him through our fellow creatures and our sense-experience of the natural world. But Sarah Ruth Cates, in declaring the supremacy of the verbal over the visual, seems to share the Reformation belief that

---

[2] In discussing the Protestant rejection of nature, and the choice of verbal over visual experience, Georgia Christopher writes: "Though a Reformed poet could not present an encounter with God as visual experience, a Catholic poet could appropriate, according to the Analogy of Being, any sensuous object from real or imagined Nature to symbolize God." Georgia B. Christopher, *Milton and the Science of the Saints* (Princeton: Princeton University Press, 1982), p. 74.

man possesses an innate knowledge of God, independent of sensory things from real or imagined nature. In my reading of "Parker's Back," O'Connor seems to be articulating her problem as a writer of metaphoric fiction: should she evoke mystery or attempt to represent it? The duality that she caused to coalesce in the transcendent vision in "Revelation" separates once again, as though language should still insist on its priority. God's Face and all other mysteries are to be revealed on the last day . . . but in the meantime? O'Connor's stark laying out of a problem indicates, for me, that metaphor was her only means of seeing *and* believing.

After a violent accident (a directed accident?) in which his tractor crashes and sets a tree on fire, Parker moves, again unconsciously, in a new direction: he will please his wife by putting God on his back. If Sarah Ruth seems all will, Parker appears all instinct, guided by an incomprehensible force toward an end that is equally incomprehensible. Looking through a book of tattoo patterns, he chooses a "Byzantine Christ" and not "The Smiling Jesus" or "Jesus the Physician's Friend." (As we have seen, "smiling" and "friend" are suspect words in O'Connor's vocabulary.) Finally, Parker does not choose a face; instead he *is chosen* by a pair of eyes, a synecdoche that links this final story with one of O'Connor's very first, "The Heart of the Park," subsequently incorporated into *Wise Blood.* Here, Hazel Motes and Enoch Emory are discovered looking into a cage and the contrast between two ways of seeing makes a very early appearance. Enoch Emory insists that the cage is "empty," but Hazel Motes feels drawn by an irresistible power:

> Over in one corner on the floor of the cage, there was an eye. The eye was in the middle of something that looked like a piece of mop sitting on an old rag. He

squinted close to the wire and saw that the piece of mop was an owl with one eye open. It was looking directly at Hazel Motes.

Enoch anticipates other characters who will find the world an empty place, and at his best he can see only the thing itself; he cannot recognize the mysterious power that Motes finds acting through things.

"That ain't nothing but a ole hoot owl," he moaned. "You seen them things before."

O'Connor's synecdoche makes the experience of both Hazel Motes and O. E. Parker doubly indirect: the part standing for the whole but the whole standing for the mystery that empowers the whole. Thus O'Connor's language mediates between a picture and a presence.

In "Parker's Back," an articulate silence ultimately overpowers both word and image, the language itself: "On one of the pages a pair of eyes glanced at him swiftly. Parker sped on, then stopped. His heart appeared to cut off; there was absolute silence. It said as plainly *as if* silence were a language itself, GO BACK." The encounter with mystery, at the same time an encounter with metaphor, affects Parker profoundly, but as *felt power*, not as meaning: "He sat there trembling; his heart began slowly to beat again *as if* it were being brought to life by a subtle power." Later, spending the night in a mission, Parker recollects the flaming tree and the possessive eyes of the Byzantine Christ—not as visual or auditory images, but as *feeling*. The *eyes* speak, but without sound. The eyes look, and though he cannot recall "the exact look of those eyes . . . he could still feel their penetration." O'Connor's prose makes its home within the province of poetry, which according to Wordsworth, treats "things

not as they *are*, but as they *appear*, not as they exist themselves, but as they *seem* to exist to the *senses*, and to the pas-
sions."[3] The "rapture" that Parker felt when he first encountered the tattooed man returns, and his disease seems
cured: "his dissatisfaction was gone, but he felt not quite
like himself. It was *as if* he were himself a stranger to himself, driving into a new country though everything he saw
was familiar to him, even at night." Parker's encounter with
mystery both alienates him from his natural self and simultaneously introduces him to a renovated natural world.

However, when at the end he brings the gift of his new
self and his new tattoo to his wife, no revelation ensues. The
exchange between the two renews the conflict between
O'Connor's ways of seeing and representing:

"Don't you know who it is?" he cried in anguish.
"No, who is it?" Sarah Ruth said. "It ain't anybody I
    know."
"It's him," Parker said.
"Him who?"
"God!" Parker cried.
"God? God don't look like that!"
"What do you know how he looks?" Parker moaned.
    "You ain't seen him."
"He don't *look*," Sarah Ruth said, "He's a spirit. No
    man shall see his face."
"Aw listen," Parker groaned, "this is just a picture of
    him."
"Idolatry," Sarah Ruth screamed. "Idolatry. . . ."

The story concludes with Parker being beaten by his wife
and reduced to an infantile state. His violent engagement

[3] William Wordsworth, Essay Supplementary to the Preface to the *Lyrical
Ballads*.

with mystery ends with *cries* and *moans* and *groans*. His only knowledge is the knowledge that he has acted and been acted upon: "he only knew that there had been a great change in his life, a leap forward into a worse unknown, and that there was nothing he could do about it."

Parker's unutterable name, his minor version of the unutterable name of God, suggests the artist's need to conceal and not declare the mystery inhabiting a story. Until the end, Parker names God only once, after his accident when he exclaims: "GOD ABOVE!" an exclamation that partakes of profanity as much as reverence. To name a mystery, as Sarah Ruth names God, is a verbal act O'Connor avoids for the most part in her fiction. We violate the author's silence by reading into her text what she took considerable pains to exclude: the direct naming of God. In a draft of "Parker's Back," she wrote: "He felt like some fragile thing of nature, turned into an arabesque of colors that only himself and the Lord could see."[4] However, in revising she cut out "the Lord" and wrote instead: "He felt like some fragile thing of nature, turned into an arabesque of colors, a garden of trees and birds and beasts." Direct naming, the "plain sense," as Donne calls it, must in O'Connor's indirect or metaphoric art bow to the "figurative God." Although the author can present the "haphazard and botched" *fact* of man's fallen nature, she can move it toward perfection only by metaphor: "one perfect arabesque of color." A lord of her own creation, the writer must keep her own secrets.

When William Blake asked the prophets Isaiah and Ezekiel how they could directly apprehend God, Isaiah replied: "I saw no God, nor heard any, in a finite organical perception; but my senses discover'd the infinite in every thing,

[4] The Flannery O'Connor Collection at Georgia College.

and I was then perswaded and remain confirm'd; that the voice of honest indignation is the voice of God. I cared not for consequences but wrote."[5] Flannery O'Connor creates her visionary poetics, uniting her with those who do not name but *see* the infinite in every thing. Before her reader can be "turned" toward the absolute, he must engage with the metaphoric process because the thing itself, whether word or image, remains inert until acted upon. To Mrs. Shortley, a peacock is a mere object—"nothing but a pea-chicken"—whereas to the poet and her implicated reader the object can be transfigured: "The peacock stood still *as if* he had just come down from some sun-drenched height to be a vision for them all." Seeing is believing, but believing is not necessarily seeing. Although the fundamental Christian Mystery of the God-Man undoubtedly influenced O'Connor's narratives, she finds it revealed in various forms, as the "mystery of personality," for example, or even as the "mystery embodied in a novel." She wrote:

> The peculiar problem of the short-story writer is how to make the action he describes reveal as much of the mystery of existence as possible. He has only a short space to do it in and he can't do it by statement. He has to do it by showing, not by saying, and by showing the concrete—so that his problem is really how to make the concrete work double time for him.

To *show* but not to *say*: the double terms of metaphor were her means of escaping from the confines of the concrete, the dead end of *vraisemblance*.

When O'Connor attempted to represent the mystery of evil in her fiction, however, she ran into unfortunate diffi-

⁵ William Blake, "The Marriage of Heaven and Hell," *The Collected Poetry and Prose of William Blake*, p. 38.

culties in "showing the concrete." How could she bring this sublime mystery into a world of action? Her given world (the fundamentalist South) and her limited range of experience provided her with meager representatives for what she had in mind. Believing that evil is "not simply a problem to be solved, but a mystery to be endured," O'Connor nevertheless went about solving the problem of picturing or demonstrating it for her readers. The danger inherent in this venture was that any particular example could reduce a mystery to some local and trivial instance. Henry James could have warned her:

> One had seen, in fiction, some grand form of wrongdoing, or better still of wrong-being, imputed, seen it promised and announced as by the hot breath of the pit—and then, all lamentably, shrink to the compass of some particular brutality, some particular immorality, some particular infamy portrayed: with the result, alas, of the demonstration's falling sadly short.[6]

In O'Connor's work, the mystery of evil too often assumes the form of venial Southern fundamentalist sins: smoking, drinking, gambling, and sex.

Edgar Allan Poe, another writer she admired and a master of suggestiveness, could have further shown O'Connor the weakening effect of illustrating evil. In "William Wilson," Poe tried to concretize Wilson's evil: "the horror and the mystery of the wildest of all sublunary visions." Wilson moves from venial sin to profound evil, and at the beginning of the tale Poe evades direct representation by assertion: he has engaged in "unparalleled infamy"; because of his "ungovernable passion," he has suffered "unspeakable misery"

[6] Henry James, *The Art of the Novel: Critical Prefaces*, ed. R. P. Blackmur (New York: Charles Scribner's Sons, 1953), p. 176.

and committed "unpardonable crime." Deliberately avoiding detail in recounting his hero's degeneration, Poe remains convincing until Wilson approaches his nadir, and then we discover that his mysterious debaucheries consist of drinking wine ("and other and perhaps more dangerous seductions"), card-playing, and profanity; near the very end, we are told that Wilson is not above seducing "the beautiful wife of the aged and doting Dr. Broglio." Poe pictures Wilson's ultimate evil act: cheating at cards. Sublime evil must suffer trivial representation. It would appear that Poe's idea of evil, no matter how grand in the imagination, had its pedestrian base in his undergraduate escapades at the University of Virginia. Poe does not report actual verbal exchanges between Wilson and his virtuous double, but emphasizes that he remains "in secret communion with my own spirit." Only in attempting to make evil concrete does Poe dissipate his ambiguity, leaving behind not an enigma but a catalogue of venial sins that hardly seems to warrant the character's unredeemable state: "dead to the world, to Heaven and to Hope!" At the end of the story Poe admits the impossibility of naming mystery ("but what human language can adequately portray *that* astonishment, *that* horror which possessed me at the spectacle then presented to view?"), but his sublimity has already been undermined by his Southern "puritanism."

Conscious of the danger of making the mystery of evil "particular," Henry James attempted in "The Turn of the Screw" to keep his evil ambiguous, to give the reader's imagination free rein in creating its own mystery. But whereas O'Connor brings mystery into her fiction as an active "presence," James provides only *reactions* to the idea of mystery. "My values are positively all blanks," James wrote,[7] but he could not give the reader a blank page on which to compose his own fiction. James's problem was how to make fictional or imaginative truth compatible with what he called "indispensible history." Referring elsewhere to the climax of Poe's *Narrative of A. Gordon Pym*, James laments the "want of connexions," of "relation," that could keep mystery from becoming merely abstract, with no demonstrated effect on human consciousness.[8] The governess in "The Turn of the Screw" may create neurotic fictions, but she is not unaware of her method: "I had restlessly read into the facts before us almost all the meaning they were to receive from subsequent and more cruel occurrences." For James, the facts are before us and we must acknowledge them even while clouding them with mystery, whereas Poe aspires to a mystery without "connections" or any "relation" to fact. William Wilson asserts: "Yet in fact—in the fact of the world's view—how little was there to remember."

As in many of James's works, the ultimate mystery of "The Turn of the Screw" is probably sexual, and James's conscious attempt to avoid particulars, to keep evil obscure, carries its own liabilities. For example, the sinister Peter Quint's death can be explained "superficially at least" as an accident. He probably had drunk too much and consequently fell down. However, James must continue to explain, rather, to insinuate: "but there had been matters in his life, strange passages and perils, secret disorders, vices more than suspected, that would have accounted for a good deal more." Young Miles is dismissed from school because he probably stole some letters, but that pedestrian fact would deflate the mystery, so James hints at intimacies with

[7] Henry James, *The Art of the Novel*, p. 177.
[8] Henry James, *The Art of the Novel*, pp. 256-257.

Quint that are not to be disclosed. And neither is the rumored sexual liaison between Quint and the former governess, Miss Jessel. Mystery in "The Turn of the Screw" consists almost exclusively of sexual innuendo; the supernatural remains powerless to transform character, as it does in O'Connor. Miss Jessel, degraded by her intimacy with Peter Quint, had a mysterious fall. The housekeeper comments on her vague ruin after leaving the household: "And afterward I imagined—and I still imagine. And what I imagine is dreadful." The governess responds: "Not so dreadful as what I do." Whereas Poe's "puritan" vices of drinking, gambling, cursing, sexual dalliance fail to accommodate the powerful and sublime mystery of evil, James's "puritan" fear of representing sexual acts causes him to evade rather than to transform his "facts." In calling "The Turn of the Screw" his "potboiler," James realized that he demanded no profound displacement on the part of his readers, perhaps no deeper concern than we bring to the reading of current mystery stories. He had engaged an absent mystery.

Just as she turns an ordinary facial expression, a smile, into a metaphor for a state of inner being, O'Connor pressed the ordinary fundamentalist "vices" of smoking and drinking into service as signs of a more profound corruption. In her drafts of "The Train," the early story that was to become a part of *Wise Blood*, Hazel Motes smokes and drinks, but revision takes away these bad habits. He appears clearly in contrast to Asa Hawks, the devil's representative, who both smokes *and* laughs, doubly authenticating his evil: "He lay down on the cot and finished the cigarette; his face was thoughtful and evil. Once while he was lying there, he laughed and then his expression constricted again." In the dining car, Hazel Motes is seated with three women; they have painted fingernails and one blows smoke in his face while another laughs. In what is surely a residual detail belonging to the earlier version of the character, O'Connor shows Motes making a cigarette after he leaves the diner, but he never smokes it; in fact, the author specifies that he never smokes or drinks. By indirection these "vices" belong to the social world he has outgrown. When he was in the army he paid his social dues by both smoking and drinking, but in his search for a more mysterious communion he discards earlier bad habits.

The materialistic and hedonistic parents of the young boy in "The River" are also characterized by their smoking and drinking. Mrs. Connin, the babysitter, announces the household's corruption as soon as she enters: "I couldn't smell those dead cigarette butts long if I was ever to come sit with you." When drinking indicates a "violent" rejection of community, however, it can be made positive and can even become a sign of integrity. Thus in "The Comforts of Home," Sara Ham defies conventional decorum and shatters the passivity of her well-established superiors. She is the individual who will not conform: "Come get this girl! Come get her! Drunk! Drunk in my parlor and I won't have it!" Likewise Parker, in "Parker's Back," drinks alone, hoping to block out the mysterious force that has been pursuing him all his life. He enters a pool hall—one of the very few collective bodies in all O'Connor's fiction—but not to share in any camaraderie. Already drunk, Parker apparently suffers a lingering need to hold onto some aspect of shared fellowship, but he is beaten up and tossed out of the group. Moreover, when he goes home, he has to face a bitter known, in contrast to a threatening unknown: his humorless wife, who does not "smoke or dip, drink whiskey, use bad language or paint her face." When drinking indicates individual defiance of conventional behavior and not social pleasure, O'Connor can turn drunkenness into a metaphor, suggesting, in Blake's proverb, that "the road of excess leads to the palace of wisdom."

In her compelling need to figure forth the mystery of evil, O'Connor in her final novel, *The Violent Bear it Away*, evades overt representation by giving the devil a voice but no *bodily form*; however, she allows him to assume other appearances, as the schoolteacher Rayber and, most violently, as the "friendly" rapist at the end of the book. The disembodied voice first speaks as a "stranger" but later it becomes the voice of a "friend," and later a "dear friend," suggesting once again the progressive dangers O'Connor saw in worldly attachments. After his great-uncle's death, young Tarwater has to find his way in the world alone, and he recalls the old man's warning:

> "You are the kind of boy," the old man said, "that the devil is always going to be offering to assist, to give you a smoke or a drink or a ride, and to ask you your bidnis. You had better mind how you take up with strangers. And keep your bidnis to yourself."

The "stranger" tempts Tarwater to look on his life as lonely, without value, spent in an "empty place." In effect, he tempts him to see without metaphor. When Tarwater mutters that he is "redeemed," the voice asks, "Do you smoke?" Although this juxtaposition seems bathetic, the smoking motif continues throughout the novel as one means of illustrating the evils of social engagement. When he goes to live with the schoolteacher in the city, Tarwater cannot maintain a fixed image of Rayber: "It was *as if* the schoolteacher, like the devil, could take on any look that suited him." However, one thing is clear: Rayber consistently smokes cigarettes. He wishes to introduce Tarwater to a "normal life," i.e., a life of smiling conformity, but the image Rayber himself projects is unnerving, recalling the woman on the train who blew smoke into Hazel Motes's face:

> Rayber took a package of cigarets from his shirt pocket and lit one, his motions inordinately slow from the effort he was making to calm himself. He blew the smoke straight into the boy's face. Then he tilted back in the chair and gave him a long hard look. The cigaret hanging from the corner of his mouth trembled.

Shortly after his great-uncle dies, young Tarwater gets drunk in an attempt to escape his destined mission of baptizing Rayber's idiot son. Again, O'Connor distinguishes between social drinking and a drunkenness that contains a violent but solitary reaction to the overpowering demands mystery places upon us. Unlike the social acts that characterize the parents in "The River," Tarwater's drinking unites him with his dead uncle whom the companionable voice is quick to criticize:

> And don't think he wouldn't heat up like a coal stove to see you take a drop of liquor, he added. Though he had a weakness for it himself. When he couldn't stand the Lord one instant longer, he got drunk, prophet or no prophet.

The voice goes on to say:

> A prophet with a still! He's the only prophet I ever heard of making liquor for a living.
> After a minute he said in a softer tone as the boy took a long swallow from the black jug, well, a little won't interfere. Moderation never hurt no one.

Here the drinking metaphor takes on a complexity and

ambiguity that reaches beyond O'Connor's usual stock "puritan" distrust of physical pleasures. Like Blake in *The Marriage of Heaven and Hell*, O'Connor approaches mystery through irony. However, unlike Blake's devil who subverts reason, O'Connor's speaks with the *reasonable* voice of society, telling us to avoid extremes, adjust to social norms, eschew violence. Whereas Blake's devil recommends breaking reasonable social bonds and freeing the God within, O'Connor's devil advocates compromise, a coming to terms with the public world, a world emptied of mystery. Moderation can *hurt* whenever it makes us feel at home in society, unconscious of the inordinate demands of mystery. O'Connor assigns Blake's "infernal sense" to characters like Tarwater and Rufus Johnson, who rage against the community's voice of common sense and moderation. These nonconformists choose for their spokesman Blake's devil who says, "You never know what is enough unless you know what is more than enough."

That the cultivation of excess can bring both a new kind of vision (at the cost of sacrificing familiar comforts) underlies the climactic scene of *The Violent Bear it Away*. The voice of the stranger, which entered the form of the schoolteacher Rayber, now becomes the stranger-friend who picks up young Tarwater when he is waiting by the highway. Tarwater, who "hungered now for companionship," ironically finds it in a sexual pervert with "delicate, pink skin." In what is probably her most unconvincing attempt at personifying the mystery of Evil, O'Connor brings into play all of the Bible-Belt "vices" that she earlier used to represent worldly corruption. The "devil" with his "lavender eyes" arrives in a "lavender and cream-colored car" and wearing a "lavender shirt." (Previously she uses the color to identify the hypocrite and social conformist, Onnie Jay Holy in *Wise Blood*: "Onnie Jay took out a lavender handkerchief and held it in front of his mouth for some time.") When Tarwater wakes up, after being violated by his "friend," he discovers that his hands are tied "with a lavender handkerchief which his friend had thought of as an exchange for his hat." In her need to underscore the devil's perversity, O'Connor has not employed verisimilar detail but only stock tags for homosexuality.

The "stranger," who existed earlier only as a voice, becomes the embodied "devil" that Tarwater's great-uncle said "would give you a smoke or a drink or a ride." The young driver "had on a lavender shirt and a thin black suit and a panama hat. His lips were as white as the cigaret that hung limply from the side of his mouth." True to form, he introduces Tarwater to smoking (in this case apparently marijuana) and to a whiskey that seems to be drugged. Having lost his will, Tarwater shortly loses consciousness and the stranger rapes him by the roadside. In her desperate need to "picture" the mystery of evil, O'Connor has been unable to do little more than duplicate Poe's illustrations. Perhaps both writers had limited experience to draw upon as resources for picturing evil, and since they momentarily abandoned their poetic suggestiveness and the indirection of metaphor (particularly O'Connor's *as if*) they produced what James rightly called the "deplorable presentable instance."

Although O'Connor provides the stage props, however, she wisely leaves the violent event undescribed. Since her paramount concern was with how superficial evil can bring about internal good, she now leaves behind the squalor of direct representation and returns Tarwater to the natural world, but with his vision quickened. The necessary violence shocks him not into knowledge but into a poetic apprehension. His physical rape has not destroyed his innocence but made him alert to the mystery that inhabits the natural world, waiting to be recognized. For O'Connor seeing without metaphor is a kind of death, making us blind to the life behind or within phenomena. O'Connor resurrects Tarwater to the presence of the unknown while alienating him from the known:

> It was the road home, ground that had been familiar to him since his infancy but now it looked like strange and alien country.

Having purged Tarwater of his need for others, O'Connor abandons her need to reproduce actuality, *things-as-they-are*. Arming Tarwater with provident metaphor, she can free herself from "ordinary" transcription:

> His scorched eyes no longer looked hollow or *as if* they were meant only to guide him forward. They looked *as if*, touched with a coal like the lips of the prophet, they would never be used for ordinary sights again.

The metaphoric extravagance that ends *The Violent Bear it Away* contrasts with the imagery of evil drawn from the social world. O'Connor's general distaste for existing society caused her to substitute bad habits for profound evil, but she was able to transcend her personal limits by creating a mysterious configuration of words. Since the social world provides the raw materials for most traditional novels—a world in which people smoke and drink and sleep together—we can understand why O'Connor was more at home in "that realm which is the concern of prophets and poets."

In her attempts to imagine the mystery of evil, O'Connor failed to avoid what James called "the deplorable presentable instance," but her failure came about not simply because she lacked a cosmic sense of evil. Well before her, Coleridge's readers were disturbed by a similar incongruity when the poet represented the Ancient Mariner's interior evil by his shooting of a bird and his goodness by his blessing of water snakes. Both Coleridge and O'Connor were far more concerned with motives than with images, which are made significant only by what they conceal. A violent "bad" act no more proves evil than good works prove goodness. In "A Memoir of Mary Ann," O'Connor alerts her readers to the difficulty of penetrating the disguises (sometimes trivial) that good and evil can take, and she implies that the writer needs realizing metaphors rather than softening clichés:

> Few have stared at that [the good] long enough to accept the fact that its face too is grotesque, that in us the good is something under construction. The modes of evil usually receive worthy expression. The modes of good have to be satisfied with a cliché or a smoothing-down that will soften their real look.

The "real look" of good or evil remains invisible, mysterious; but the process, the coming into being, can be witnessed by a writer who evolves herself as she constructs her characters. The end of such a process will be "revealed" at the end of time, but in time metaphor is our means of discovery, as these early lines from *Wise Blood* attest:

> The black sky was underpinned with long silver streaks that *looked like* scaffolding and depth on depth behind it were thousands of stars that all *seemed* to be moving

very slowly *as if* they were about some vast construction work that involved the whole order of the universe
and would take all time to complete [my emphasis].

Thus O'Connor's "good" appears to be that power working in or behind phenomena but also within us, recreating
the self, uniting man and nature in a spiritual evolution that
language cannot explain, only indirectly point toward. Evil,
on the other hand, either denies or arrests that process.
Like Blake, O'Connor seems to believe that all act is virtue
and that evil only negates, "hindering of act in another." In
contrast to the good under construction, evil is constructed,
fixed, adjusted to things as they are (to existing social forms
and material fact), blind to mystery—the made-up mind divorced from feeling. Since our evolution must begin with
what is worst in us, we find that almost all O'Connor's characters are guilty of some transgression that interrupts their
development. Often they are self-satisfied and believe
themselves self-sufficient; they pretend to control and order
their lives and the lives of others around them. Trapped in
selfhood, they sometimes strive (like Sheppard in "The
Lame Shall Enter First" and Rayber in *The Violent Bear it
Away*) to retard another's movement toward fullness of
being.

Hence, no actions in isolation from the process revealed
by the fiction can be accounted good or evil; since the process is moving toward ultimate good, a morally reprehensi-
ble person can be an agent for furthering the "construction"
of good. Metaphoric language aims at disclosing the process
but not at judging moral behavior, and the "omniscient"
narrator of O'Connor's fiction paradoxically works within assumed limits. The notorious Misfit in "A Good Man is Hard
to Find" or the less violent Rufus Johnson in "The Lame

Shall Enter First" are ultimately struggling agents of beneficence. Coleridge would have seen their anti-social acts as a language that we imperfectly read:

> Our Fellow-creatures can only judge what we *are* by what we *do*; but in the eye of our Maker what we *do* is of no worth, except as it flows from what we *are*. Though the Fig-tree should produce no visible Fruit, yet if the living Sap is in it, and if it has struggled to put forth Buds and Blossoms which have been prevented from maturing by inevitable contingencies of tempests or untimely frosts, the virtuous Sap will be accounted as Fruit. . . .[9]

Just as we should be wary of judging *appearance* through pre-established moral categories, we are likewise shown the dangers of using conventional aesthetic categories as reliable signs of interior value. Since the poet aims to uncover the process of coming into being, she feels compelled to redefine "beautiful" and "ugly" whenever the words substitute *appearance* for mystery. The absence of superficial beauty in O'Connor's work discomforts many of her readers who are, perhaps, looking for beautiful products rather than the beauty of process. Her notoriously unattractive characters resemble caterpillars evolving into butterflies, and as she forces our attention to a lower stage of the evolutionary process she makes us acknowledge that beauty inhabits *all* acts of becoming. By seeking out only the butterfly and ignoring the caterpillar, we run the risk of reducing the beautiful to the picturesque, in the same way that clichés mask genuine feelings. Beauty like goodness cannot be *identified*

---

[9] Samuel Taylor Coleridge, *The Friend*, ed. Barbara E. Rooke (Routledge & Kegan Paul, London and Princeton University Press, Princeton, 1969), II, 314.

with an object—a person or objects in the natural world; it is a way of seeing an object. The grandmother in "A Good Man is Hard to Find" seems blind to both art and nature. She calls attention to a scene, but she cannot see it: "Oh, look at the cute little pickaninny! . . . Wouldn't that make a picture, now? . . . If I could paint, I'd paint that picture." To the unseeing eye, even poverty is picturesque.

Early in *Wise Blood*, the unattractive Sabbath Lily tells a story about a woman with good looks who tried to get rid of her ugly child. But the child kept returning, until the woman and her lover "strangled it with a silk stocking and hung it up in the chimney."

> "It didn't give her any peace after that, though. Everything she looked at was that child. Jesus made it beautiful to haunt her. She couldn't lie with that man without she saw it, staring through the chimney at her, shining through the brick in the middle of the night."

> "My Jesus," Haze muttered.

> "She didn't have nothing but good looks," she said in the loud fast voice. "That ain't enough. No sirree."

More than one reader has been offended by O'Connor's refusal to create pleasant images, comforting similes like Eudora Welty's. One reader finds her view of life "repugnant,"[10] not only because she writes about unappealing people but because she compels her readers to embrace them in spite of—or rather, because of—their ugliness. Like goodness, beauty can be released from its physical confinement by metaphor; and, by directing our attention to a lower stage of an evolutionary process, O'Connor ensures

[10] Martha Stephens, *The Question of Flannery O'Connor* (Baton Rouge: Louisiana University Press, 1973), p. 3.

that, undistracted by appearances, we will begin to recognize a power that supersedes all aesthetic categories. Good looks are truly not enough; it is the mysterious power "shining through the brick in the middle of the night" that rescues us from the confining forms of materialism. If, as Roman Guardini says, "Evil is what is absolutely superfluous," then the beautiful power of goodness is that it is absolutely essential. By her cultivation of the ugly, O'Connor keeps us from *identifying* ourselves with the material. Instead, a piece of passing description can awaken us to the power *within* the natural world: "The trees were full of silver-white sunlight and the meanest of them sparkled." The power, capable of "shining through the brick in the middle of the night," inhabits the trees, making them sparkle. The meanest of O'Connor's characters sparkles as well.

Accepting an essentially flawed human nature, O'Connor questions the value of superficial beauty, as she does the value of all appearances. The "beauty contest" that takes place in "The Partridge Festival" seems as trivial as the town's motto ("Beauty is Our Money Crop") is materialistic. Like a prophet, O'Connor combats the dangerous illusion that good looks—like good works—are enough, and she further refuses to tolerate our contentment with ourselves as we are—and not as we can be. At times, O'Connor resembles Gulliver after his return from Brobdingnag, when he cannot look in a mirror without comparing his inferior physical image with that of the superior giants he remembers. O'Connor shares Gulliver's wonder and laughter at human pride and absurdity, but she also keeps in mind the lesson in perspective Gulliver learned from his travels: "Our beauty is only apparent; our disproportion real."[11]

[11] Samuel Holt Monk, "The Pride of Lemuel Gulliver," *The Sewanee Review*, LXIII (1955), p. 61.

As I pointed out earlier, many of O'Connor's characters can be characterized by their limited vision. Some see only what meets the eye, and their inability to see metaphorically tells us that the author will very shortly devise some violent means of opening their eyes. Often confining and liberating viewpoints are juxtaposed. We have seen how Hazel Motes detects an overpowering presence in a cage at the zoo while his companion Enoch Emory remarks, "That ain't nothing but a ole hoot owl." The peacock in "The Displaced Person" brings about a similar confrontation and in this case natural beauty and human ugliness are also juxtaposed:

> "So *beauti-ful*," the priest said. "A tail full of suns," and he crept forward on tiptoe and looked down on the bird's back where the polished gold and green design began. The peacock stood still *as if* he had just come down from some sun-drenched height to be a vision for them all. The priest's *homely* red face hung over him, glowing with pleasure.
>
> Mrs. Shortley's mouth had drawn acidly to one side. "Nothing but a peachicken," she muttered [my emphasis].

Just as the roadside trees mentioned earlier were "full of silver-white sunlight," the peacock's tail is "full of suns"; and as the meanest of the trees sparkled, the priest's homely face is glowing. One more instance of contrasting ways of seeing occurs in "A View of the Woods." To a young girl, the woods provide more than a picturesque "view":

> She stared across the lot where there was nothing but a profusion of pink and yellow and purple weeds, and on

across the red road, to the sullen line of black pine woods fringed on top with green. Behind that line was a narrow gray-blue line of more distant woods and beyond that nothing but the sky, entirely blank except for one or two threadbare clouds. She looked into this scene *as if* it were a person that she preferred to him.

To her grandfather, the woods are only a collection of trees, a material possession to be used or sold. The girl tries to persuade him that something will be lost with the "view"—a way of seeing and not just the thing seen. But the old man, blinded by selfishness, finds only the material world:

> The old man looked across the road to assure himself again that there was nothing over there to see. "I never have seen you act in such a way before," he said in an incredulous voice. "There's not a thing over there but the woods."

For O'Connor, as for Wordsworth, the thing itself, whether man or a natural appearance, is impoverished without an informing power that beautifies every thing in the process of becoming more than itself.

In "The Temple of the Holy Ghost," the only one of her stories directly concerned with Roman Catholics and Catholic ritual, O'Connor seems to me only nominally to deal with the Incarnation. She again demonstrates how metaphor can lead to a metaphoric reality in which customary beauty and ugliness are transcended. When two cousins from a convent school come for a visit they ridicule a nun's saying that their bodies are Temples of the Holy Ghost. But the young girl of the house (who has fat cheeks and braces and always "acts ugly") has not yet reached the stage at which one thinks it wise to disparage metaphoric thinking and maintain a clear distinction between an empirical fact (the body) and an imaginative fiction (a temple). The girl says to herself, "I am a Temple of the Holy Ghost," and the metaphor pleases her: "It made her feel *as if* somebody had given her a present." The original meaning of the Greek word for grace, *charis*, is "the release of beauty." Despite her pride, which makes her "deliberately ugly to almost everybody," the young girl inhabits an acute metaphoric reality, and she is capable of creating fictive roles for herself, as war hero (even her sex can be transformed) or saint. Although her consciousness wavers and her religious convictions appear uncertain, the child witnesses the effect of metaphor. Secure in the privacy of her bedroom, after her cousins leave for a fair, she looks out of her window:

> At regular intervals a light crossed the open window and threw shadows on the wall. She stopped and stood looking out over the dark slopes, past where the pond glinted silver, past the wall of woods to the speckled sky where a long finger of light was revolving up and around and away, searching the air *as if* it were hunting for the lost sun. It was the beacon light from the fair.

Earlier, the child happily accepted an identity—"I am a Temple of the Holy Ghost"—but now we find O'Connor creating a more energetic metaphor, suggesting that man, alienated in a fallen world, continually seeks restoration of his lost power. Immediately after this figurative excursion, however, the actual fact—"it was the beacon light"—asserts itself. The poverty of an empirical identity ("nothing but a ole hoot owl"; "nothing but a peachicken"; "There's not a thing over there but the woods") follows the metaphoric light that throws shadows, causes the pond to sparkle—a power actively "revolving," "searching," "hunting." The participles contrast with the mere statement of equation. The intensity of the metaphor (the lost sun) foreshadows the symbolic sun at the end of the story, which while struggling to overpower things-as-they-are still maintains affinity with the actual. Within a spectrum of associations, the child can begin to contemplate the source of light; through metaphor, she can engage the mystery. However, direct apprehension of the meaning of experience, divine or literary, remains unbearable: "With her hair blowing over her face she could look directly into the ivory [the Host's color] sun which was framed in the middle of the blue afternoon but when she pulled it away from her eyes she had to squint."

When the young cousins return from the fair, they report that they have seen a freak, a radical deviation from all conventional ideas of beauty that brings the norm itself into question. Earlier in the story, O'Connor demonstrated the illusory character of physical beauty: "The lanterns gilded the leaves of the trees orange on the level where they hung and above them was black-green and below them were different dim muted colors that made the girls sitting at the table look prettier than they were." The lanterns suggest fanciful rather than imaginative power, artifice rather than the sun's creating; and their feeble, superficial distortions pale beside the fundamental distortion suffered by the hermaphrodite. If the child's body can contain the Holy Ghost, perhaps the hermaphrodite embodies metaphor itself, bringing together the opposites that, since Plato, have been hungering to join. Metaphor, a verbal condition contrary to fact, includes the pride of the child and the humility of the hermaphrodite, who declares: "This is the way He wanted me to be and I ain't disputing His way." Although the child can accept a metaphor—herself as a Temple—she cannot comprehend the *fact* that two sexes can be one. Only in her imagination (presented by O'Connor as a later "dream") can she reconcile the freak of nature and her Church's doctrine (to the "understanding" equally freakish).

Next day, when the cousins return to the convent school, the child reluctantly goes to the chapel for benediction. Far from doctrinaire, O'Connor describes only an *emerging* consciousness, when the child's "ugly thoughts stopped and *she began to realize* that she was in the presence of God" [my emphasis]. Beauty, like goodness, is ever about to be. An incipient poet, the child, in effect, creates a metaphor that marries incompatible entities, the mystery of the Host *represented as an image* before her and the hermaphrodite's words, which she imagines into the scene: "when the priest raised the monstrance with the Host shining ivory-colored in the center of it, she was thinking of the tent at the fair that had the freak in it. The freak was saying, 'I don't dispute hit. This is the way He wanted me to be.' " The beautiful "Host shining ivory-colored" mysteriously mingles with the grotesque—i.e., to the superficial eye, the ugly.

Because the child's evolving consciousness mirrors the writer's own, the story does far more than demonstrate the efficacy of Paul's teaching. The monstrance becomes only one aspect of a syncretistic symbol: sun, monstrance, freak, Holy Ghost, child. Consequently, the young girl does not enjoy a beatific vision uncorrupted by things of this world; she returns home with a driver who "smells" and has "pointed ears almost like a pig's." She returns to a world of resemblances, to a referential reality, where images are distinguished by means of *like* and *as*, and are still to be symbolically united:

The sun was a huge red ball like an elevated host drenched in blood and when it sank out of sight, it left a line in the sky like a red clay road hanging over the trees.

O'Connor ends the girl's (and her own) symbolic reach and restores her to "normal" relationships, more customary ways of seeing. Despite its import as mysterious Host (the zenith of its fictive amplitude) the sun returns to its bodily self, the "lost sun" that the beacon light was searching for. The sun has merged with the Host but what it leaves behind *resembles* a red clay Georgia road.

O'Connor shares with many modern poets a mistrust of the word beautiful. In "Good Country People," Mrs. Hopewell laments that her "bloated, rude and squint-eyed" daughter has changed her "beautiful name" Joy to Hulga, which she finds "the ugliest name in the language." The names themselves contrast the girl's perverse need for an individual identity with her mother's desire for social harmony: the agreeable manner, the "pleasant expression." Even the word "joy" in Mrs. Hopewell's vocabulary suggests self-satisfaction more than the overpowering force of bliss or rapture. Mrs. Hopewell would disguise and subordinate the self in order to conform to things-as-they-are, a beauty of surfaces. Looking at her daughter, she thinks: "There was nothing wrong with her face that a pleasant expression wouldn't help." And the author underscores Mrs. Hopewell's basic dishonesty: "Mrs. Hopewell said that people who looked at the bright side of things would be beautiful even if they were not." Mrs. Hopewell's clichés, the common coin of social exchange, confine her to a temporal community and block her way toward the recognition of Mystery. In this relatively early story, O'Connor presents unproductive extremes. Hulga, disillusioned, contemptuous of her surroundings, has "achieved" blindness. By not paying "any close attention to her surroundings," she alienates herself from the power operating within nature and can therefore "see through to nothing." And her mother, who cannot penetrate surfaces, sees nothing beyond.

The same opposing pair—the "stylish lady" and the fat, scowling daughter who has "ugly looks for everybody"—appears in O'Connor's masterful later story, "Revelation," but here the false opposition is mediated by Ruby Turpin, a third character who holds center stage, and who discovers the life-giving power that lies behind all natural and social forms. Although we will look at this story later, in connection with O'Connor's endings, here we can point out that mystery can come to life only when customary ways of seeing beauty and ugliness are disrupted. With a "friendly smile," Ruby Turpin, like Mrs. Hopewell, accepts the demands of a polite society, its hierarchy and conventions, but when she begins to doubt the value of her social identity, she starts a movement that can free the mystery confined by superficial forms, whether natural or linguistic.

> What if Jesus had said, "All right, you can be whitetrash or a nigger or ugly!"

> Mrs. Turpin felt an awful pity for the girl, though she thought it was one thing to be ugly and another to act ugly.

Within prescribed limits, Mrs. Turpin will entertain some displacement in the chain of being, but she does not anticipate a change of species: her antagonist Mary Grace causes her to ask not "Am I a hog?" but "How am I a hog?" Even the adage she uses, "One thing to be ugly and another to act ugly," resonates with more than the obvious plea for social adjustment: *acting ugly* in the world's eyes is a metaphor for the violence necessary to alter consciousness and to begin the evolution toward true beauty and goodness, and *appearing* ugly has no verifiable correlation with ugliness of being. Only Satan *is* ugly—and he cannot be described except by images that trivialize his power.

Like Coleridge's Ancient Mariner, who by his violent tale of suffering alienates the Wedding Guest from his comfortable social role, ugly Mary Grace through her violent act teaches Ruby Turpin that beauty is not a stable surface to be appreciated but a hidden power that demands the destruction of social and linguistic preconceptions before it can be seen. Believing that she has achieved immunity from the world's ugliness through her good works and proper behavior, Ruby finds even her clichés disproved. "It never hurt anyone to smile" is belied by the "angry red swelling above her eye"; and Ruby Turpin with the "friendly smile" will be scowling like Mary Grace when she returns home: "Claud slept. She scowled at the ceiling." However, even before she reaches home, Ruby knows that her way of seeing has been radically altered. Her secure definition of beauty has been violated:

> As their pick-up truck turned into their own dirt road and made the crest of the hill, Mrs. Turpin gripped the window ledge and looked out suspiciously. The land sloped *gracefully* down through a field *dotted* with lavender weeds and at the start of the rise their *small* yellow frame house, with its *little flower beds* spread out around it like a *fancy* apron, sat *primly* in its *accustomed* place between two giant hickory trees. She would not have been startled to see a burnt wound between two blackened chimneys [my emphasis].

O'Connor describes both a physical place and a condition of

being, and Ruby Turpin's beautiful has been exposed as the pretty, the picturesque. The imagined "ugly" violence threatens only the feeble, ephemeral shapes she has imposed on the world. Ruby's expanding vision even burns through the false piety of her Negro help who attempt to reinforce the status quo, her earlier sense of beauty as social conformity: "You des as sweet and pretty as you can be" and "Jesus satisfied with her." Both Ruby's satisfaction with appearances and her self-satisfaction have been altered, as a preparation for her apocalyptic vision that arrives at the story's end.

By undermining the value of beautiful and ugly as terms for realizing the mystery of human existence, O'Connor opens the way to apocalypse. In her quest to reach beyond human assessments of human worth, she felt compelled to expose all phantom representations of interior being. The two Roman Catholic priests who very briefly figure in her body of work are far from idealized: one has a "homely red face" and is absent-minded, if not senile; the other is blind in one eye, deaf in one ear, and has a "grease spot on his vest." O'Connor wrote to a friend: "Maryat's niece asked her why I made Mary Grace so ugly. Because Flannery loves her, said Maryat. Very perceptive girl." Natural objects are not beautiful without our attention or, in Blake's words, "Where man is absent, nature is barren." By implicating her readers in her own love for ugly misfits, O'Connor introduces us to the process of seeing, and thereby provides a kind of redemption for flawed images. Mother Teresa said of her job of caring for the ugly, diseased, and dying of Calcutta: "It's beautiful work." Metaphor is the poet's work of seeing, its own cause and its own effect, and it is independent of the body of nature, whether called ugly or beautiful.

Thus, we may conclude that the word mystery, like any word, is defined by a context, not by a dictionary, and the word's effect depends on the person approaching it, the qualifying eye. To social psychologists like Sheppard in "The Lame Shall Enter First" or Rayber in *The Violent Bear it Away*, it is an "idiot mystery" they cannot "explain" away. Mystery disturbs most of O'Connor's characters, and it becomes an "ugly mystery" to Mr. Fortune in "A View of the Woods" whose materialistic "view" reduces the woods to mere lumber: "A pine trunk is a pine trunk."

Mr. Fortune possesses his land, and would even possess his own granddaughter, by imposing his own identity, his own name, on her. O'Connor's metaphor "works" to bring him into an engagement with a "presence" he has ignored. In a remarkable passage, she mingles the imagined and the actual, the power external to the self and the *things* at hand:

> The third time he got up to look at the woods, it was almost six o'clock and the giant trunks *appeared* to be raised in a pool of red light that gushed from the almost hidden sun setting behind them. The old man stared for some time, *as if* for a prolonged instant he were caught up out of the rattle of everything that led to the future and were held there in the midst of an uncomfortable mystery that he had not apprehended before. He saw it, in his hallucination, *as if* someone were wounded behind the woods and the trees were bathed in blood. After a few minutes this unpleasant vision was broken by the presence of Pitt's pick-up truck grinding to a halt below the window. He returned to his bed and shut his eyes and against the closed lids hellish red trunks rose up in a black wood.

Mr. Fortune finds the mystery both uncomfortable and unpleasant. In a rather pointed allusion to the crucifixion, O'Connor urges his unacknowledged need to the level of consciousness, but in his "hallucination" the blood becomes confused with evil, "hellish red trunks." Resisting what he cannot rationally comprehend, he is a "figure on the threshold of some dark apocalypse," to use O'Connor's description of Rufus Johnson in "The Lame Shall Enter First." However, by denying the presence within and behind nature, he wakes to the "presence" of a pickup truck, a part of the "rattle of everything." A truck's power substitutes for supernatural power. Subsequently, in anger and frustration, Mr. Fortune kills his granddaughter, finds himself deserted in a remote place, and suffers a heart attack. The final two sentences of the story activate mystery and juxtapose his need for "someone" external to the self with a counterfeit "presence," a yellow bulldozer that feeds on the material world.

> On both sides he saw that the gaunt trees had thickened into mysterious dark files that were marching across the water and away into the distance. He looked around desperately for someone to help him but the place was deserted except for one huge yellow monster which sat to the side, as stationary as he was, gorging itself on clay.

The process of spiritual evolution initiated by Mary Fortune's violent act (resembling Mary Grace's violent act in "Revelation") reaches no conclusion. Mr. Fortune's realization, his recognition of his own inadequacy, comes tragically too late. His growth has been arrested because he has allied himself with fixity, a created and not a creating power.

In the passage quoted above, Flannery O'Connor's *as if* construction confers on her character Mr. Fortune the good fortune of self-realizing metaphor. In a surprisingly short time, she changes him from a person who believes that a "pine trunk is a pine trunk" to one who sees things that *appear*, things that look *as if* they were other. (The "almost hidden sun" suggests the threshold that is the base of metaphor.) The *as if* offers imaginative access to the unknown, a bridge between veristic resemblances and the ultimate substance of all of O'Connor's fiction: apocalyptic power, that which for convenience we call mystery. Mr. Fortune only *looks* and *stares* at the woods—his vision confines him to a world of mere objects—but O'Connor awakens him to a power hidden behind or within objects, that is also within himself: "the old man stared some time *as if* for a prolonged instant he were caught up out of the rattle of everything that led to the future and were held there in the midst of an uncomfortable mystery that he had not apprehended before." O'Connor's metaphor creates a violent, almost intolerable, disruption in what she calls elsewhere "ordinary sights." Mr. Fortune both *sees* and sees *as if*: "He saw it, in his hallucination, *as if* someone were wounded behind the woods and the trees were bathed in blood." By juxtaposing two ways of seeing (what Blake called single and double vision) and linking them by *as if*, O'Connor presents to the reader an avenue between the two, a "medium between the literal and the metaphorical" that can be called symbol. In her story "Circe," Eudora Welty allows her goddess to comment on human mystery: "I tell myself that it is only mystery, and mystery is only uncertainty." O'Connor's mystery is no blur, but a certain, defining power; no puzzle to be figured out, but a vital organic process, involving all mankind. Every cliché of thought or language provides a defense against mystery, but every act, even an evil one (which Augustine defined as a "swerving of the will") can ultimately further the evolution of a higher consciousness. Even Iago realizes that it is not Cassio the object that is beautiful, but the power that invests his life:

> He hath a daily beauty in his life
> That makes me ugly.

Because Iago has *seen* the beauty in Cassio's life, he has perhaps begun the process of his own regeneration. O'Connor's metaphoric acts bring her reader into contact with mystery, often painfully, by breaking his independent spirit, severing his ties with others, and sending him into temporary exile. But finally they serve to make him recognize that he is on his way home.

Events crowd and push and nothing happens.
        — CONRAD

No end to this. — FLANNERY O'CONNOR

IV

MAKING AN
END

In her story "Greenleaf," Flannery O'Connor created one of
her typical matriarchs, fearful of the unknown and reso-
lutely determined to make her earthly "place" secure. Mrs.
May sees herself as a good person, whose virtue shows in
the charitable works she performs for others, particularly
the Greenleaf family. She speculates that it would be ironic
if, after all her efforts, one of the Greenleaf children should
sue her for injuries his father suffered on her farm: "she
thought of it almost with pleasure as if she had hit on the
perfect ending for a story she was telling her friends." The
perfect ending for Mrs. May is an ironic one and her delight

derives from imagined incongruity: that good works do not necessarily produce good results, that cause and effect can be disconnected, that the satisfying ending may be the least expected, a surprise, if not a shock. Certainly Mrs. May's speculation ironically foreshadows the ending of "Greenleaf" itself, when she will die on the horns of a bull, but the author may also be confronting, in an oblique way, the matter of literary form. O'Connor customarily had no trouble beginning her stories, but she did not always, like Mrs. May, "hit on the perfect ending." Even though she had the conclusion in mind as she was writing "Greenleaf," she did not know how she would give this event resonance, how meaning could be revealed. Her religious "belief" provided no cure-all for the anxieties attending the making of metaphors. O'Connor early mastered the skill of capturing local character, and her ear for dialogue was acute, but the knowledge that life ends in death does not resolve the problems of fictional meaning and form. The church may teach us how to die, but not how to write. O'Connor sent *The Violent Bear it Away* to her editor, not certain of whether it was a novel or a collection of individual stories, and as usual uncertain of her ending: "I've rewritten the last pages so I'll enclose them as I think they're an improvement. When the grim reaper comes to get me, he'll have to give me a few extra hours to revise my last words. No end to this."

If at times the denouements of O'Connor's stories seem inexplicable and arbitrary, the reader should not, in my view, relieve his fictional anxiety by resorting to the concept of "Grace" as O'Connor's *deus ex machina*. Neither should he convert the author's deliberate uncertainty into a certain statement: "Greenleaf," according to one critic, represents "the spiritual debilitation of the work ethic,"[1] and for an-

---

[1] Shannon Burns, "Flannery O'Connor: the Work Ethic," *The Flannery O'Connor Bulletin*, VIII (1979), p. 59.

other (taking a psychological approach) the bull "is one of those bad men," who threaten the men in O'Connor's South who are "either diseased, infantile or murderers."[2] The straining after referential equivalences for a poet's metaphors retards their process of growth, their ability to carry a heavy workload of various, even contradictory, meanings. O'Connor wrote to "A.": "I am very happy now writing a story in which I plan for the heroine, aged 63, to be gored by a bull. I am not convinced yet that this is purgation or whether I identify myself with her or with the bull." Of course, in the situation of metaphor, she is both.

Since O'Connor accepted the Christian "fact" that death ends existence but not life, she went about using death as a controlling metaphor; however, her literary problem was how to create aesthetically satisfying endings that do not foreclose the possibility of continuation. Rejecting a return to the human community offered by comedy, and denying that suffering ends in tragedy, O'Connor was left with two verbal strategies for concluding a narrative: (1) through irony imply a necessary transforming power (as Eliot did in *The Waste Land*), or (2) through metaphor show that same power acting within external nature and imaginative vision. In either case, man's relation to a social world loses its priority, and language, not belief, becomes the material out of which to forge a temporal end for narratives. By looking at the ending of "Greenleaf" and subsequently at the ending of her two novels, and two other short stories, separated by a decade, we can discover how O'Connor worked variations on a central paradigm. The primitive Christian church ritual may have used formulaic endings for its prayers, but a literary artist must do constant battle with fixity, the made-up mind that finds its expression in cliché. "I try militantly,"

[2] Josephine Hendin, *The World of Flannery O'Connor* (Bloomington: Indiana University Press, 1970), p. 115.

O'Connor wrote, "not to be affected by the pious language of the faithful."

If O'Connor had been content with creating mere illustrations of a preconceived truth—elaborate allegories—she would have known what the bull in "Greenleaf" stands for and would not have had to discover its significance through writing. From the opening sentences, however, the author will not allow the bull to remain a static sign: "Mrs. May's bedroom window was low and faced on the east and the bull, silvered in the moonlight, stood under it, his head raised as if he listened—like some patient god come down to woo her—for a stir inside the room." Immediately the writer begins fabricating disguises for power, the unknown power that can assume a variety of verbal forms. After personifying the bull and associating it with pagan myth, O'Connor turns it into a synecdoche for a violent nature encroaching on the human realm, an erotic force that threatens decorous behavior, the jealous Old Testament God demanding loss of self as a precondition of being. The bull becomes symbolically all of these, as well as a bullet, a snake, a stone, the sun. Well before Mrs. May encounters the bull, she comes upon Mrs. Greenleaf in a religious frenzy, "sprawled obscenely on the ground," and the sound of her incantation becomes another form for mysterious power: "The sound was so piercing that [Mrs. May] felt as if some violent unleashed force had broken out of the ground and was charging toward her." This obvious foreshadowing has a more immediate effect: through metaphor the woman (and the reader) has experienced the story's "conclusion." The appearance of the literal bull only confirms a metaphorical engagement that has already taken place. Unfortunately, the failure to recognize the import of verbal experience has fatal consequences for the principal character.

In contrast to Mrs. May, who fears any violent engagement, Mrs. Greenleaf remains accessible to imaginative experience, and her articulated metaphors contrast vividly with Mrs. May's suppressed emotions. Mrs. Greenleaf welcomes a threat to her own selfhood: " 'Jesus, stab me in the heart!' and she fell back flat in the dirt, a huge human mound, her legs and arms spread out as if she were trying to wrap them around the earth." The intense, sexual metaphors, openly engaged, place Mrs. Greenleaf in opposition to Mrs. May, with her propriety and her passive acceptance of the orthodox chain of being: "Mrs. May felt as furious and helpless as if she had been insulted by a child. 'Jesus,' she said, drawing herself back, 'would be *ashamed* of you.' " Scandalized Christianity offends other O'Connor characters, like Mrs. McIntyre in "The Displaced Person" ("Christ in the conversation embarrassed her"), but perhaps the Devil in *The Violent Bear it Away* best represents a proper and debilitated Christianity, with his ironic proverb: "Moderation never hurt no one."

Not only does Mrs. May hide herself behind conventional social and language forms but she also finds comfort in her own image, which, like Narcissus, she finds reflected from the natural world. She has outlawed the violent "other" that is real for Mrs. Greenleaf, and thus her needs are pacified by pleasing analogies with the created world, undisturbed by an embarrassing creator: "The pastures were enough to calm her. When she looked out any window in her house, she saw the reflection of her own character." As the story develops, O'Connor steadily undermines Mrs. May's self-satisfied control. On a visit to the Greenleaf's milking room, Mrs. May "felt as if she were going to lose her breath." She cannot directly confront the sunlight that brightens the room, and here O'Connor may be suggesting that all language, whether couched in satisfying analogies or violently disturbing metaphors, must finally fail. That which is external to words triumphs, as in Kafka's aphorism: "our art is dazzled blindness before the truth: the light on the grotesquely distorted face is true, but nothing else is."[3] Unable to bear intensity, Mrs. May remains outside the milking room, but she cannot exclude from her awareness the destructive force that is on the way. She becomes "conscious that the sun was directly on top of her head, like a silver bullet ready to drop into her brain." Although O'Connor labors to evade any direct presentation of the actual sun, even when made particular through analogy, she prefigures the event that will close her story. She has educated her heroine to the ways of metaphoric thinking by blinding her to representational language. In an extravagant display of rhetorical energy, she builds up the metaphoric power that is the writer's only way of evoking the non-verbal power within man and nature. The action occurs, of course, in the dream-imagination:

> Half the night in her sleep she heard a sound as if some large stone were grinding a hole on the outside wall of her brain. She was walking on the inside. . . . She became aware after a time that the noise was the sun trying to burn through the tree line and she stopped to watch, safe in the knowledge that it couldn't, that it had to sink the way it always did outside of her property. When she first stopped it was a swollen red ball, but as she stood watching it began to narrow and pale until it looked like a bullet. Then suddenly it burst through the tree line and raced down the hill toward her. She woke up with her hand over her

---

[3] Kafka's comment appears in Erich Heller, *The Disinherited Mind* (New York: Meridian Books, 1959), p. 200.

mouth and the same noise, diminished but distinct, in her ear. It was the bull munching under her window.

Although we may tend to agree with the critic who claims that "language is much more largely referential in the novel than in other literary forms,"[4] we must be wary of O'Connor's settings and dialogue because they only *seem* to reproduce actuality. Her essential language works at disrupting or undermining the value of physical representation. Just as Mrs. May becomes disoriented, so does the reader. In poetry as prophecy, character, plot, setting, and speech all serve the writer's subversive design on the reader's customary ways of seeing the world. Paul Ricoeur could have had O'Connor's fiction in mind when he wrote, "Everything takes place as if logical absurdity had replaced analogy in the explanation of metaphor."[5]

In Mrs. May's dream, the noise outside is inside. The sun burning, through synesthesia becomes a stone grinding on her brain. Protean, the sun turns into a ball and then a bullet and only upon Mrs. May's waking into the thing itself. At last, *the thing itself!* Needless to say, the author has given very little attention to the bull as an animal. When the story reaches its end, we may hunger for a final resolution, a Joycean epiphany in which self-recognition produces momentary aesthetic stasis. But with O'Connor the words conceal far more than they reveal. Both Mrs. May and the bull are killed, but both are expendable when we realize that they were only a means of engaging metaphor. If we feel, as one reader does, "deliberately shut out from the final, and thus the overall, experience of the story,"[6] it may be because we have failed to recognize that the story's experience is an ex-

---

[4] Ian Watt, quoted in David Lodge, *The Language of Fiction* (New York: Columbia University Press, 1966), pp. 26-27.

[5] Paul Ricoeur, *The Rule of Metaphor*, p. 191.

[6] Martha Stephens, *The Question of Flannery O'Connor*, p. 40.

perience of metaphor which tells us not what happened in the unmediated world of fact, but what is always happening within the evolving consciousness. O'Connor's conclusion to "Greenleaf," like that of most of her other stories, glorifies the unknown but refuses to assume God-like omniscience. Her metaphors are finally metaphors of displacement. In responding to one critic of his own inconclusive endings, Chekhov wrote, "but you are confusing two concepts: *answering the questions* and *formulating them correctly*. Only the latter is required of an author."[7]

The ending of "Greenleaf" hovers between a declaring prose and an ambiguous, obscuring poetry. Here are the final lines of the story, which I have reshaped in order to highlight two differing uses of language, although some mingling of modes occurs:

[The bull] was crossing the pasture	as if he were overjoyed to find her again.
She remained perfectly still,	not in fright, but in a freezing unbelief.
She stared at the violent black streak . . .	as if she had no sense of distance,
	as if she could not decide at once what his intention was,
and the bull had buried his head in her lap,	like a wild tormented lover . . .
One of his horns sank until it pierced her heart. . . .	

[7] Anton Chekhov, *The Letters of Anton Chekhov*, trans. Michael Henry Heim and Simon Karlinsky (New York: Harper and Row, 1973), p. 117.

She continued to stare
    straight ahead

but the entire scene in
front of her had
changed—the tree line
was a dark wound in a
world that was nothing
but sky—

and she had the look of a
person whose sight has
been suddenly restored
but who finds the light
unbearable.

She did not hear the shots
    but she felt the quake in the
    huge body . . .

she seemed . . . to be
bent over whispering
some last discovery into
the animal's ear.

The straightforward beginning of sentences gives the illusion of a reportorial accuracy, but the writer at once qualifies each declarative by a figurative evasion, unsettling our hold on verisimilar truth. As we have seen with the Misfit in "A Good Man is Hard to Find," the interior life that remains hidden behind appearances is made vital by the poet's metaphors: the pervasive *as if* and *seems*. Although the "omniscient" author shares with her readers what Mrs. May *hears* and *feels*, she will not share with us Mrs. May's "last discovery." Like the Oracle at Delphi, she neither reveals nor conceals, but gives signs.

Flannery O'Connor was well aware that death could become a cliché of structure, a means of stopping without concluding. Death concludes a character's consciousness of events, but it does not always provide a satisfactory end for a writer's metaphoric impulse. Only if death has been inherent in the fictional life can it serve as the culmination of a story; otherwise it is a way out, not a way in toward meaning. Probably because the idea of death was paramount in O'Connor's personal life, she could easily project it onto every fictional situation she created. She wrote to J. F. Powers: "after thirty pages death is the great temptation." Refusing to make overt statements of belief that are incompatible with narrative movement, O'Connor used death as a means of bringing actual existence and meaning into temporary collaboration. Because death in her fiction is another metaphor, she can create representations that people find incredible. Thus watching the film adaptation of *Wise Blood*, spectators were repelled near the end when Hazel Motes murders Solace Layfield. Seen as figurative enactment, on the other hand, the death can be accepted as the end of Motes's double or false self. O'Connor has again undermined pure representation.[8] Likewise the Misfit's murder of a whole family in "A Good Man is Hard to Find" would be intolerable, even meaningless, as "realism." The Misfit makes murder a figure of speech when he says, "She would of been a good woman, if it had been somebody there to shoot her every minute of her life." The unbalanced killer thinks metaphorically, and we might as appropriately say of Mrs. May: she would of been a good woman if it had been a bull to gore her every minute of her life. In my view, the most common difficulties in reading O'Connor come about from looking out of the text toward the real world for validation of behavior and toward religious doctrine for verification of meaning.

Many of O'Connor's stories end in death: in some, a survivor remains to endure the pain of loss and begin a move-

---

[8] Paul Ricoeur rightly declares that "what happens in poetry is not the suppression of the referential function but its profound alteration by the workings of ambiguity." Paul Ricoeur, *The Rule of Metaphor*, p. 224.

ment toward an enlarged consciousness; in others, the reader is left to carry on the evolution in his own mind. Only one story in the group we are considering, "The Lame Shall Enter First," resembles conventional tragedy, in which articulated self-knowledge accompanies death. Sheppard, like Creon in *Antigone*, represents the prideful hero convinced that he possesses "the truth." He would strip all disguises from mystery, but he meets his match in Rufus Johnson, a misfit whose antisocial behavior resembles Antigone's. The battle between verifiable truth and religious mystery ends when Sheppard's child dies and the father acknowledges that he bears the responsibility: "His heart constricted with a repulsion for himself so clear and intense that he gasped for breath. He had stuffed his own emptiness with good works like a glutton. He had ignored his own child to feed his vision of himself." Rarely in O'Connor's work can we find a moral position so firmly taken or a more blatant assertion of meaning. This anomalous approximation of the tragic mode dispenses with O'Connor's customary ambiguity. The unambiguous ending stabilizes meaning and leaves no door open.

A far more typical confrontation with death occurs at the end of "Everything that Rises Must Converge," when the author rejects the stability of a single meaning. Two victims of illusion—a mother, Mrs. Chestny, and her son, Julian— cannot see beyond appearances, but when she is knocked down by a black woman, they both become radically disoriented: "she seemed to be trying to determine his identity" and very shortly "he was looking into a face he had never seen before." O'Connor takes what is superficially a racial incident and makes it resonate with inexplicable meaning, even though the young man, like a self-assured critic, believes himself capable of comprehending what lies hidden behind appearances: " 'What all this means' he said, 'is that the old world is gone.' " His "explanation of its meaning," however, fails to come near the truth, and as his mother collapses, he discovers not ideas but feelings, while she, apparently dead, attains no translatable knowledge at all.

Like the young girl in "A Circle in the Fire," who "stares up at her mother's face as if she had never seen it before," Julian must suffer derangement before he can begin to move toward self-knowledge. In his irrational cry, "Mamma, Mamma," he returns to a world of need, but one innocent of meaning, a world he has not *seen* because of his blind pride. His mother appears "as if the spots of light in the darkness were circling around her," but like meaning itself the source of light is withheld from both Julian and the reader:

> . . . he cried and jumped up and began to run for help toward a cluster of lights he saw in the distance ahead of him. "Help, Help!" he shouted, but his voice was thin, scarcely a thread of sound. The lights drifted farther away the faster he ran and his feet moved numbly as if they carried him nowhere. The tide of darkness seemed to sweep him back to her, postponing from moment to moment his entry into the world of guilt and sorrow.

In striking contrast with the ending of "The Lame Shall Enter First," this figurative ending imposes no values on the situation. Once arrogant in asserting the "meaning" of experience, Julian becomes inarticulate and directionless. Perhaps O'Connor may be obliquely commenting on the limitations of her language resources: in unfolding the interior life, narrative is dispensable and metaphor can only *promise* significance. The story fails to reach an end, because Julian is metaphorically "nowhere," but by being divorced from imposed meaning, he is free to begin moving toward the meaning that was always there. As Wallace Stevens said, echoing Plato, "not to have is the beginning of desire."[9] The ending maintains the duality of O'Connor's vision, like the face of Julian's mother: "One eye, large and staring, moving slightly to the left as if it had become unmoored. The other remained fixed on him, raked his face again, found nothing and closed." Like O'Connor, Mrs. Chestny has one eye on the material world, the world of physical resemblances that finally come to nothing; the second one on another realm summoned by the *as if*, where human consciousness is released from its confining forms. Julian, too, caught between two states of consciousness, must wait—even for his suffering. The participle "postponing" accurately sums up O'Connor's coming into being and her prospective endings.

Faced with a suspended ending, a door left ajar, we sometimes resort to social science or psychology in hopes of importing an explanation for human behavior into the text. O'Connor's unsettling endings encourage what Coleridge called "the tendency to look abroad, *out* of the thing in question, in order by means of some *other* thing analogous to understand the former. But this is impossible—for the thing in question *is* the act we are describing."[10] In various readings, Julian's mother is a reactionary snob who gets her comeuppance; Julian an arrogant, upstart liberal finally brought to his knees; the black woman is sympathetic or unsympathetic depending on the reader's own attitude toward disfranchised Southern minorities. But since O'Connor's

[9] Wallace Stevens, "Notes Toward a Supreme Fiction," *Collected Poems* (New York: Alfred A. Knopf, 1954), p. 382.
[10] Samuel Taylor Coleridge, *Collected Notebooks*, vol. III, 4225.

disinterested eye spares none of her three characters, we should be alert to the need to look beyond "real" characters as our chief means of discovering fictional truth. Character, according to C. H. Rickword, is "merely the term by which the reader alludes to the pseudo-objective image he composes of his responses to an author's verbal arrangements. Unfortunately, that image once composed . . . can be criticized from any angle and its moral, political, or religious, significance considered, all as though it possessed actual objectivity, were a figure of the inferior realm of real life."[11] Although this statement may savor of "Living? Our servants can do that for us," it nevertheless seems a necessary corrective to more "realistic" readings. But however we approach "Everything that Rises Must Converge," the figurative and non-figurative meanings remain incompatible. Julian shouts, but makes "a thread of sound"; his feet move but "as if they carried him nowhere"; "the lights drift farther away," and the tide of darkness only *seems* to sweep him back toward his mother. O'Connor's metaphors have unmoored her characters from time and space. Reality's flow is not stopped, only arrested for a moment in words. Commenting on Chekhov's endings, one reader remarked that Chekhov leaves before the meal is over. More profoundly antisocial, O'Connor may leave before the meal has begun.

The successful irresolution of "Everything that Rises Must Converge," in which a way of seeing dominates what is seen, can be highlighted by looking at an unsuccessful story, "The Enduring Chill," in which O'Connor struggled to give the Holy Ghost a local habitation and a name. In relating O'Connor's story to Flaubert's "A Simple Heart," my

[11] C. H. Rickword, "A Note on Fiction," in Edgell Rickword, *Essays and Opinions: 1921-1931*, ed. Alan Young (Cheadle Hulme, Cheadle, Cheshire, England: Carcanet New Press, 1975), p. 233.

aim is not to disparage a story that she herself did not like, by placing it next to an acknowledged masterpiece, but to illuminate her recurring difficulty with endings. In "The Enduring Chill" O'Connor aspired to bring literary imagination and Christian doctrine into a happy collaboration, if not a marriage.

O'Connor began the story in early November, 1957, and a couple of weeks later, she thought it was finished, except for "a month of revisions," but in early December she wrote to Caroline Gordon: "I'm busy with the Holy Ghost. He is going to be a waterstain—very obvious but the only thing possible." By mid-December, she was clearly frustrated: "I have torn the story up and am doing it over or at least a good deal of it over. . . . I haven't got it right yet." Half of the next year was spent improving it, and even after it appeared in *Harper's Bazaar* (July, 1958), O'Connor wrote to Maryat Lee:

> When I read that last paragraph in print I knew instantly that it was too long. When I have another collection, I am going to do some operating on it before I put it in. The problem was to have the Holy Ghost descend by degrees throughout the story but unrecognized, but at the end recognized, coming down, implacable, with ice instead of fire.

The author continued to express dissatisfaction with the story at intervals during the next six years, and even when Robert Giroux, her editor, was assembling the stories that would constitute her posthumous collection *Everything That Rises Must Converge*, she remained troubled: "There is considerable rewriting I want to do on the one called 'The Enduring Chill,' so you might wait to put that in galleys until I get the new version." Near the very end of her life, in mid-July, writing to Catherine Carver, she accepted failure: "I don't much like it but I am afraid once I get to messing with it, I'll make it worse than it is." By early August she was dead.

Once more, we discover that O'Connor's concerns as a writer are less with the credibility of her character's performance than with how her metaphors perform. Unfortunately, in the case of "The Enduring Chill," she apparently deviated from her customary poetic practice by predetermining her meaning; rather than allowing her sign (a water stain) to refer to a reality outside of language, she strained to will it into a theological concept and, at the end of the story, deserted the ambiguity central to metaphor for the certainties of direct statement. In effect, she denies the reader the possibility of alternate responses to the same figure, whereas Flaubert, in marked contrast, labors to prevent a *single* response.

At the beginning of "The Enduring Chill," the young man Asbury returns home to die; rather, he is under the illusion that he is dying. Ignorant of his ignorance, he plans to make his mother "face reality" and assume responsibility for thwarting his artistic development. In her first paragraph O'Connor's irony makes the reader realize that Asbury is no artist. Rather than using his imagination to look *into* the given world, he desires an "exotic" fiction, an escape from what he sees as an impoverished reality. The sun is "like some strange potentate from the east" and a "strange light" seems to disguise or evade things-as-they-are.

Asbury felt that he was about to witness a majestic transformation, that the flat roofs might at any moment turn into mounting turrets of some exotic temple for a god he didn't know.

The exotic temple in Georgia is our immediate sign that Asbury's pride will be stripped away, along with his pretentious illusions. Since she had her ending clearly in mind, O'Connor only needed to prepare for it, as Allen Tate suggested, by getting the Holy Ghost into the early parts of the story. Thus she writes that she is "busy with the Holy Ghost," for her difficulty was in bringing Him, and not her character Asbury, to life.

William Blake believed that any abstraction (the Enlightenment's "reason") is a Spectre, the satan of the visionary artist. If so, we find O'Connor battling with her Spectre, trying to embody a theological concept in a physical text. She imagines Asbury in New York where he meets a priest named "Ignatius Vogle, S.J."—a less than subtle association with the Dove—who explains to Asbury:

> "There is," the priest said, "a real probability of the New Man, assisted, of course," he added brittlely, "by the Third Person of the Trinity."

After he is home and confined to his bed, Asbury asks to see a priest so that he can discuss intellectual and artistic matters, and another illusion shatters when the priest says that he has never heard of James Joyce. However, what the priest does know concerns, not surprisingly, the Holy Ghost, and he tells Asbury that he "must pray to the Holy Ghost," and that "God does not send the Holy Ghost to those who don't ask for him." Asbury has felt that his mission was to make his mother "see herself as she was," but the priest strongly asserts that it is Asbury who is ignorant and without vision: "The Holy Ghost will not come until you see yourself as you are." The theological concept has by now been made explicit and O'Connor can begin, through metaphor, to dramatize the Spirit in action.

O'Connor describes the ceiling stain that must temporarily house the mysterious power that threatens Asbury's selfhood and the "illusions" that keep him in ignorance. Ceiling leaks have made a stain that *resembles* "a fierce bird with spread wings" and we learn that in the past Asbury was troubled by its ominous power:

> It had been there since his childhood and had always irritated him and sometimes had frightened him. He often had the illusion that it was in motion and about to descend mysteriously. . . .

As we approach the ending, O'Connor must give the appearance of life to the waterstain, quicken it by metaphor, and paradoxically indicate that its power is *not* illusory. Employing her customary language devices, she indicates that the bird *seemed* poised above his head and that looking at the bird he *felt* "it was there for some purpose that he could not divine." Even his eyes look *as if* "they had been prepared for some awful vision about to come down to him." These poetic evasions reach their culmination when the water stain-bird *appeared* "all at once to be in motion." As a Christian must avoid the pantheistic heresy of identifying God with his creation, so the poet O'Connor must keep from saying that the water stain *is* the Holy Ghost. But two kinds of illusion have been compounded: O'Connor's fictional illusion that serves as her means of reaching knowledge merges with Asbury's bogus illusion which precludes knowledge. Through words such as *seems*, *felt*, *as if*, and *appeared* O'Connor has constructed an ambiguous language structure that can be destroyed only by the *fact* of direct statement. Her story ends:

> The boy fell back on his pillow and stared at the ceil-

ing. . . . The old life in him was exhausted. He awaited the coming of new. It was then that he felt the beginning of a chill, a chill so peculiar, so light, that it was like a warm ripple across a deeper sea of cold. His breath came short. The fierce bird which through the years of his childhood and the days of his illness had been poised over his head, waiting mysteriously, appeared all at once to be in motion. Asbury blanched and the last film of illusion was torn as if by a whirlwind from his eyes. He saw that for the rest of his days, frail, racked, but enduring, he would live in the face of a purifying terror. A feeble cry, a last impossible protest escaped him. But the Holy Ghost, emblazoned in ice instead of fire, continued, implacable, to descend.

More than Asbury's "film of illusion" has been torn away; if, as O'Connor writes, he has "failed his god, Art," perhaps she by her direct engagement with the implacable spirit, fails art too. In contrast to "A Temple of the Holy Ghost," in which the girl's body, a freak, and the Holy Ghost are united in a metaphoric family, here her *as if* bows to the static verb *to be*. Phrases such as "like a warm ripple" and "as if by a whirlwind" are overpowered by *was*: "the old life in him was exhausted," "it was then that he felt," "it was like," the "illusion was torn from his eyes." Only the word *appeared* remains to shadow us from blinding truth. Implacable doctrine has overpowered fictional illusion, exposing the "meaning" that O'Connor in her other stories manages to keep hidden behind metaphor. By equating her representation with a single meaning, she closes off possibility. By directly naming the Holy Ghost, she diminishes his power in fiction.

Like Flannery O'Connor, Gustave Flaubert began "A

Simple Heart" with an idea: to tell the story of a parrot, Lou-lou, and end with "the apotheosis of the parrot." As his story progressed, however, Flaubert began to concentrate on Félicité, a simple peasant woman in whose imagination the parrot was to become the Holy Ghost. Ignorant of doctrine but humble before mystery, Félicité never doubts what she cannot explain; for her the Holy Ghost is not a threat (as it is for O'Connor's Asbury) but the peaceful consummation of a life spent feeling His presence. Flaubert's aversion to religious dogma is as well known as O'Connor's submission to it, but the two writers share the problem of building a cage for Loulou, a structure that can house the Holy Ghost. Both endings are in themselves grotesque, if not laughable. The technical challenge was how to insinuate the Holy Ghost into the mind of a character but also into the reader's mind so that the supernatural appears somehow credible in fiction. Apparently, neither writer anticipated the extent of the difficulty of both preparing for a transcendent vision and of displaying it in a final paragraph. Both were courting an apocalypse. Flaubert said, *"Il faut finir ma Félicité d'une façon splendide."*[12]

Lacking even a rudimentary education, Félicité neither affirms nor denies, since both positions demand that some intellectual order be imposed on the world. Her innocence includes an innocent eye, the capability of seeing a world in a grain of sand. Unlike O'Connor, who needs to shock Asbury into awareness, Flaubert had only to reward Félicité for unquestioning acceptance of her experience. However, to keep her beatitude from becoming sentimental, he needed to strengthen her character by showing her ability to transform her outer world of things into symbols of her

---

[12] Gustave Flaubert, quoted in George A. Willenbrink, *The Dossier of Flaubert's "Un Coeur Simple"* (Amsterdam: Editions Rodopi, 1976), p. 235.

interior life. Because she can detect the mystery shared by all created things—the hidden power that O'Connor also engages—Félicité continually unifies the disparate images and events that constitute her life. Rather than entertaining the Holy Ghost as a concept, she sees only His *evidence*, and her syncretic imagination permits the Spirit to assume various forms such as breathing, fire, and even a lowly bird. By showing her confusing (or confounding) her parrot Loulou with the Holy Ghost, Flaubert assigns her a supreme power of imagining a whole where others face only separate parts. Like a poet, she refuses to subordinate image to idea, representation to concept. The two terms of metaphor are made compatible.

In one early version of his story, Flaubert has Félicité confess to a priest that she has been worshipping a parrot instead of the Holy Ghost, and the priest tries to clarify the nature of idolatry; but Flaubert soon cut the episode and through numerous revisions added further examples of Félicité's creative power, a power made possible by her unconscious rejection of logical thinking.[13] One of Flaubert's additions may suffice:

> In church she was always gazing at the Holy Ghost in the window and observed that there was something of the parrot in him. The likeness was still clearer, she thought, in a crude color-print by Epinal representing the baptism of Our Lord. With his purple wings and emerald body he was the very image of Loulou.
>
> She bought him, and hung him up instead of the Comte d'Artois so that she could see them both together in one glance. They were linked in her

---

[13] In my commentary on "A Simple Heart," I am depending heavily on the material assembled by George A. Willenbrink.

thoughts; and the parrot was consecrated by his association with the Holy Ghost. . . . And though Félicité looked at the picture while she said her prayers she turned a little from time to time towards the parrot.

(*A l'église, elle contemplait toujours le Saint-Esprit, et observa qu'il avait quelque chose du perroquet. Sa ressemblance lui parut encore plus manifeste sur une image d'Epinal, représentant le baptême de Notre-Seigneur. Avec ses ailes de pourpre et son corps d'émeraude, c'était vraiment le portrait de Loulou.*

L'ayant acheté, elle le suspendit à la place du comte d'Artois,—de sorte que, du même coup d'oeil, elle les voyait ensemble. Ils s'associèrent dans sa pensée, le perroquet se trouvant sanctifié par ce rapport avec le Saint-Esprit. . . . Et Félicité priait en regardant l'image, mais de temps à autre, se tournait un peu vers l'oiseau.)

By adding two other scenes of this sort, Flaubert celebrates the informing, coalescing power of Félicité's imagination. However, by using words such as "association," "resemblance," "rapport," and "like," he maintains a clear separation in his reader's mind. Maintaining a dual vision, Flaubert was still left with the technical problem of how to create a persuasive apotheosis. If he appeared blatantly ironical, skeptical of his character's naive vision, he would diminish the value of his own creation; if he presented her vision as revealed truth, without any ambiguity, he would desert the precincts of fiction, the world of metaphor (O'Connor's *as if*). In "The Enduring Chill," Flannery O'Connor faced a similar problem: can a writer name mystery? Can fiction point to its own transfiguration?

The manuscript changes in the last paragraph of "A Sim-

ple Heart" indicate that the questions were not easily answered. In searching for words to describe Félicité's death-
bed vision, Flaubert was working very hard to declare her
personal "truth" while maintaining his own uncertainty. He
must avoid confusion while admiring it. First he places the
parrot and the Holy Ghost side by side, with no connective
word whatever: "she sees the Holy Ghost parrot above her
smiling head" ("elle voyait le Saint-Esprit perroquet au-dessus de sa tête souriante"). In another attempt, the parrot
and the Holy Ghost, distinctly separated by a conjunction,
come together in her fading mind: "she confounds the Holy
Ghost and the parrot, hovering over her in the skies—and
dies" ("Elle confond le Saint-Esprit et le Perroquet, planant
sur elle dans les cieux—et meurt"). At one time, Flaubert
resorts to simile, having her apprehend a parrot that is *like*
the Holy Ghost. Finally, he cuts any naming of the Holy
Ghost and the last paragraph reads, in what is probably the
definitive manuscript version:

> An azure vapor rose up to Félicité's room. Her nos-
> trils met it and inhaled it with a mystical sensuality;
> then she closed her eyelids. Her lips smiled. Her
> heartbeats lessened—one by one—vaguer each time
> and softer—as a fountain subsides, as an echo van-
> ishes—and when she sighed her last breath, she be-
> lieved that she saw in an opening in the skies—a gigan-
> tic parrot—hovering above her head.
>
> (*Un vapeur d'azur monta dans la chambre de Féli-
> cité. Elle avança les narines, en la humant avec une
> sensualité mystique; puis ferma les paupières. Ses
> lèvres souriaient. Les mouvements du coeur se raeenti-
> rent—un à un—plus vagues chaque fois, plus doux—
> comme une fontaine s'épuise, comme un écho dispa-*

raît;—et quand elle exhala son dernier souffle, elle crut
voir dans les cieux entr'ouverts,—un perroquet gigan-
tesque—planant au-dessus de sa tête.)

Even after Flaubert eliminated the name of the Holy Ghost,
its presence still remains because of the meaning accumulated from earlier associations. The bird suffers no taint of
allegory; it does not stand for the Holy Ghost; it has become
a symbol that incorporates the unknown. The Holy Ghost is
implicit in language as He is implicit in the world. In the
process of his revisions, Flaubert shifted from "she saw the
Holy Ghost" to "she thought [or believed] that she saw the
Holy Ghost." When he decided to erase the Holy Ghost's
name, he was still left with His representation, and the
problem of credible "revelation" also remained. Still waver-
ing, he at last decided to evade direct confrontation altogether and to cloud the mystery that Félicité *thinks* she
sees. By preserving ambiguity, Flaubert keeps his ending
open, but, what is more important, transfers to the reader's
mind the problem of creating a personal reconciling vision.

Flannery O'Connor's urge to demonstrate mystery in the
ending of "The Enduring Chill," to name the Holy Ghost,
led her to impose rather than to discover meaning, to make
explicit what metaphor seeks to hide. At the end of "The Artificial Nigger," she gave to Mr. Head the knowledge that
the mystery he had encountered could not be translated:
"there were no words in the world that could name it."
However, on occasion her prophetic calling to tell the
Christian truth conflicts with the poet's calling to "tell all the
Truth but tell it slant." Her years of laboring over "The Enduring Chill" show how compelling was her need to stay
within the boundaries of fiction and yet, like Flaubert's Félicité, attain some ultimate unity of being. O'Connor wrote

and rewrote her endings because it was here, as in life itself, that belief collided with make-believe.

The conventional ending for comedy, marriage, is only momentarily entertained by O'Connor—and disparaged—in *Wise Blood*. However, for Hazel Motes's landlady, a creature dedicated to the material world and unconscious of mystery, marriage is a way of closing off possibility: "there's only one thing for you and me to do. Get married," she tells Hazel Motes. For her, the world is an "empty place" and marriage clearly represents not a rite but a coming together for convenience and material comfort. Her severely limited vision makes her incapable of comprehending Motes's metaphor of "backward to Bethlehem." She sees time as meaningless movement: " 'There's nothing, Mr. Motes,' she said, 'and time goes forward, it don't go backward. . . .' " Horrified, as if the forces of darkness were tempting him to accept a world without ultimate value, Hazel Motes abruptly leaves Mrs. Flood's "place," her meaningless temporality—and the novel as well. When he is found by the police, he has lost any relation with Mrs. Flood's forward-moving time: "he asked them in a hoarse whisper where he was and if it was night or day." His dislocation and disorientation would serve as a prelude to apocalyptic vision in later O'Connor works, but at this early stage she does not follow through; instead she deserts her protagonist on the threshold of being, producing an ending of the first type: through irony implying some necessary transforming power. In "The Train," the thesis story she incorporated into *Wise Blood*, Motes is left in the "rushing stillness" of the train, and with this resonant and paradoxical phrase stasis and movement were combined. Apparently unsatisfied by her first type of ending, by looking ironically at Motes, O'Connor immediately shifts to her other way of concluding:

showing a power acting in a world that, contrary to Mrs. Flood's view, is not "empty." Some would contend that the writer errs in shifting her attention to a minor character whose limited sensibility must bear the weight of the novel's accumulated meaning, but at this early stage in her writing career, O'Connor may simply have been less skillful at integrating her alternate ways of seeing. In any case, to counteract the silence that isolates Motes, language now begins transforming the raw material that is Mrs. Flood. Confronting the shell of Motes, she finds that the "eye sockets seemed to lead into the dark tunnel where he had disappeared." Since Mrs. Flood is unable to *see* the world she has adjusted to, O'Connor begins moving her toward another dimension, by means of figurative language. By emphasizing a separation between what is and what should be, irony demands cool detachment, but in order to show *positively* the changes beginning inside Mrs. Flood, language must engage with her evolving life. Looking at the dead man before her, Mrs. Flood finds the nothing that precedes true seeing: "She shut her eyes and saw the pin point of light." O'Connor's characteristic *as if* enters to awaken Mrs. Flood from the sleep of materialism:

> She felt *as if* she were blocked at the entrance of something. She sat staring with her eyes shut, into his eyes, and felt *as if* she had finally got to the beginning of something she couldn't begin, and she saw him moving farther and farther away, farther and farther into the darkness until he was the pinpoint of light.

Like Hester Prynne's tombstone, "relieved only by one ever-glowing point of light," Mrs. Flood receives but slight divine illumination, but her vision has been quickened until "she saw him moving." Although O'Connor's ultimate reality remains secure beyond words, words can mirror that "moving." The ending of *Wise Blood*—in effect, two endings, a negative and a positive one—demonstrates the difficulty of resolving a narrative when neither comedy (marriage) nor tragedy (death) makes an acceptable end. Fiction's severe demands are as exacting as apologetics', and Gide's comment on Mauriac's novels applies equally to *Wise Blood*: "The object of your novels is not so much to bring sinners to Christianity as to remind Christians that there is something on earth besides Heaven. . . ."[14]

Some ten years after *Wise Blood* came *The Violent Bear it Away*, but four years before it was published O'Connor wrote to a friend: "I have a sentence in mind to end some story that I am going to write. The character all through it will have been hungry and, at the end, he is so hungry that 'he could have eaten all the loaves and fishes, after they were multiplied.' " The hyperbole apparently precedes the story and character, although the novel must have been underway at this time. It is significant that she came upon a poetic figure as a means of effecting a close, and we recall that it was the "artificial nigger," that "wonderful phrase," that incited her to write one of her most famous stories. Tarwater, like Hazel Motes, ends up rejecting the social world, but whereas death arrests Motes's journey through time, and the rest is silence, Tarwater survives the world's rape and so makes possible O'Connor's alternative mode: to show through metaphor a transformed world and a renovated vision. Metaphor makes the familiar unfamiliar: his country "looked like strange and alien country." Actually, Tarwater's external world has not changed, but, as Blake

[14] André Gide, quoted in Conor Cruise O'Brien, *Maria Cross: Imaginative Patterns in a Group of Modern Catholic Writers* (New York: Oxford University Press, 1952), p. 6.

says, "the eye altering alters all." At the end of the novel, O'Connor's *as if* again serves as a bridge between inner vision and outer representation.

As her character's consciousness begins to stabilize, O'Connor's rhetorical tension increases. Approaching "mystery" (and meaning), the author strongly resists direct statement. Although she mentions mystery, we are left with the *sense* of a mystery that "resides" in nature, until we realize that the early portion of the sentence, the *seems*, brings the existence of mystery into question: "The encroaching dark seemed to come in deference to some mystery that resided there." O'Connor's verbal equivocation continues and her series of figures provides the only cure for Tarwater's paralysis. Thus the novel finds its conclusion in language, not in external event. Coleridge's comment on *The Faerie Queene* applies: "its domain is neither history nor geography but mental space." Finding himself "unable to go forward or back" (also an affliction of Hazel Motes), Tarwater realizes that his way lies outside of time, beyond the literal into the metaphoric. Moving out of the horizontal plane onto the vertical, his hunger, multiplied like the fishes, begins to rise: "He felt it rising . . . rising and engulfing him." He begins whirling; losing his direction, he finds it:

> There, rising and spreading in the night, a red-gold tree of fire ascended as if it would consume the darkness in one tremendous burst of flame. The boy's breath went out to meet it. He knew that this was the fire that had encircled Daniel, that had raised Elijah from the earth, that had spoken to Moses and would in the instant speak to him.

Like the boys at the end of "A Circle of Fire," Tarwater is

connected by metaphor with the book of Daniel, but whereas earlier the author gave us an authorial Biblical analogy to reinforce meaning, now the kinship is acknowledged by a character. His family is not in the world.

O'Connor seeks a way to evade the trap of linear time, and her rising, circling imagery indicates a poetry of apocalypse. However, after Tarwater's vision fades, and the divine injunction to prophesy is no longer heard, "The words were as silent as seeds opening one at a time in his blood." What remains to be told cannot be told. Narrative has been transcended. Unlike the ending of *Wise Blood*, where Hazel Motes's merger with the absolute was only implied, the ending of *The Violent Bear it Away* offers an achieved consciousness, even though the character's experience remains open. His death to the world makes possible his movement towards a goal still to be realized, and Tarwater ends *moving steadily* toward the Babylon he hopes to reform. By accepting vision and the process following vision, the *promise* of metaphor, O'Connor creates a paradigm for most of her later stories. Tarwater's interior battle has been fought and won. How he deals with the "children of God" sleeping in the city is a social concern, the material for the conventional novel O'Connor always refused to write.

O'Connor's various endings indicate not a shifting belief but a dynamic conception of artistic form, and just as her later novel shows a firmer command of fictional materials, two of her short stories may demonstrate a similar unfolding. The abrupt cessation of "The Life You Save May Be Your Own" (1952) contrasts markedly with the consummate ending of one of her very last stories, "Revelation" (1964). The earlier story depends on our viewing with humor and ironic detachment a world without spiritual value; the latter *reveals* the value-making power inherent in man *and* nature. The understatement and negative vision of the earlier story may leave behind an unproductive ambiguity, whereas the positive overstating of "Revelation" may alienate a reader who resists a prophet's "unrealistic" vision.

In "The Life You Save May Be Your Own," Mr. Shiftlet, like the Misfit in "A Good Man is Hard to Find," appears to be a man without a social context, and O'Connor's metaphor of "place" again implies mankind's need for some supernatural reality. The old woman ("ravenous for a son-in-law") attempts to anchor Shiftlet in place by marrying him to her handicapped daughter. She says, "there ain't any place in the world for a poor disabled friendless drifting man" (almost the identical speech Mrs. Flood makes to Hazel Motes near the end of *Wise Blood*), but in return for his marrying her daughter, she offers to share her "permanent place." She would own her son-in-law, just as she owns her three mountains and the sun.

Shiftlet's figures of speech seem a parody of Christian dualism, but they nevertheless indicate that he is aware of an opposition out of which meaning can arise: "The body, lady, is like a house: it don't go anywhere; but the spirit, lady, is like an automobile: always on the move. . . ." His automobile, like Hazel Motes's Essex, ironically becomes his material means of escaping materialism, his "place to be that I can always get away in." However, in *Wise Blood*, Hazel Motes's spiritual life appears authentic, whereas in "The Life You Save May Be Your Own," Shiftlet lives for his stories which conceal him from the reader and possibly from himself. He seems protean in the forms he can take, but the forms are without content. He has mastered the *rhetoric* of morality.

Although O'Connor declared Shiftlet to be "unredeemable," it is the old woman who seems without a conscience, although she does shed a few tears when Shiftlet takes her daughter away. However, in the author's general design on the world, she serves a constructive purpose: by marrying Shiftlet to innocence, she aggravates what I see as his potential awareness of need that remains buried beneath words— to be explored in O'Connor's subsequent stories. But O'Connor declines to take her character seriously; her language, which usually works to enlighten both her characters and her readers, here blocks access to the "mystery" of character.

Although Shiftlet is clearly as materialistic and dishonest as the old woman—he marries Lucy Nell solely to gain possession of an automobile—he does show ambiguous signs of an interior life that precede a change of consciousness, and almost in spite of the author's intentions. O'Connor labels his dissatisfaction "composed"; however it does persist, indicating that the money and objects he seeks do not relieve him. An unsatisfied materialist, he looks on innocent Lucy Nell and "becomes depressed in spite of the car." The progressive intensity of Shiftlet's depression could mask his birth agony, his coming into Being. Yet the author almost burlesques his spiritual deficiency, calling attention to his physical lack, his one arm. Her customary *as if* which, like metaphor, usually introduces us to the mystery behind behavior, here unmasks her character's pretension, without providing for him the possibility of self-knowledge. The *as if* only furthers a series of impressions that he is trying to create:

He seemed to be a young man but he had the look of composed dissatisfaction *as if* he understood life thoroughly.

When he starts the old car running, O'Connor ridicules his response:

> He had an expression of serious modesty on his face *as if* he had just raised the dead.

The character could be emerging into some truth about himself, but his "performance" keeps him and the reader from comprehending the possible "truth" before and within him.

> "I got," he said, tapping his knuckles on the floor to emphasize the immensity of what he was going to say, "a moral intelligence!" and his face pierced out of the darkness into a shaft of doorlight and he stared at her *as if* he were astonished himself at this impossible truth.

He may experience some genuine astonishment, some awe before the "mystery of existence," hidden behind word and gesture; on the other hand, Shiftlet may be assuming one more disguise for an identity that role-playing has erased. In any case, O'Connor abandons him before he can begin the process of becoming more than his appearances.

That Shiftlet *smokes* and has a *smile* that "stretches like a weary snake waking before a fire" might support his membership in the Devil's fraternity, but his verbal gestures are less fixed in O'Connor's scheme. Like characters in other stories, he presents a facade of words that needs to be penetrated, but O'Connor does not bring her metaphor into play, nor give Shiftlet her redeeming attention. In the above quotation, he recognizes that "moral intelligence" has value, even though his behavior appears contradictory, but we cannot be certain of what lies behind his reaction to his own phrase. Like Chaucer's Pardoner, he speaks against hypocrisy and avarice while practicing them: one is capable of possessing a "moral intelligence" without a morality.

After he abandons Lucy Nell at a roadside eating place, Shiftlet feels the need for companionship, perhaps to divert himself from the emptiness that his disguises leave behind. After declaring to a young hitchhiker that he left his mother who was an "angel of Gawd"—he parrots the words spoken by the boy in the eating place, looking at Lucy Nell—Shiftlet is visibly affected: "His eyes were instantly clouded over with a mist of tears. The car was barely moving." He may, again, be playing a theatrical game, and his sentimentality may be further evidence of a basic dishonesty, but his words *could*, like those of Thomas's mother in "The Comforts of Home," have "real experiences behind them." Like Mary Grace's violent metaphor in "Revelation," the young hitchhiker's deflating metaphors—"You go to the devil" and "my old woman is a flea bag and yours is a stinking pole cat"—leave behind a creature who, alone, has no diversions from the self. Language has exposed his pretensions, but we cannot be sure whether his apparently histrionic prayer ("Oh Lord, break forth and wash the slime from the earth") may conceal a genuine, disconsolate cry, despite his demonstrated duplicity.

In "The Life You Save May Be Your Own," the world is not charged with God's grandeur, so that mystery must be imported, but in her effort to evoke revelation O'Connor resorts to simile, natural images that make the power "within or behind" nature seem trivial. Having deprived her character of depth, she cannot shock him into recognition of even the "impossible truth" about himself. The ending, like his spiritual condition, remains unengaged.

Mr. Shiftlet was so shocked that for about a hundred

feet he drove along slowly with the door still open. A cloud, the exact color of the boy's hat and shaped like a turnip, had descended over the sun, and another, worse looking, crouched behind the car. Mr. Shiftlet felt that the rottenness of the world was about to engulf him. He raised his arm and let it fall again on his breast. "Oh Lord!" he prayed. "Break forth and wash the slime from this earth!"

The turnip continued slowly to descend. After a few minutes there was a guffawing peal of thunder from behind and fantastic raindrops, like tin-can tops, crashed over the rear of Mr. Shiftlet's car. Very quickly he stepped on the gas and with his stump sticking out the window he raced the galloping shower into Mobile.

We can speculate that by resorting to similes that reduce mystery to the ordinary or commonplace, she sacrifices for the moment the "dignifying light" of metaphor. The cloud like a turnip and the raindrops like tin-can tops give language a clear and referential function but at the cost of diminished sublimity. The turnip's descent is ludicrous and hence bathetic. Moreover, the something outside the self, the "threatened mystery of creation" only "guffaws." If the Lord answers Shiftlet's prayer, he seems to take him no more seriously than does the author.

Just as O'Connor's turnip cloud blocks out the sun, the poet has denied the reader access to either her character or to the meaning that his life may be struggling to uncover. The story stops but does not conclude. We tend to agree with Iris Murdoch that "since reality is incomplete, art must not be too afraid of incompleteness," but the ending of "The Life You Save May Be Your Own" remains unproductively ambiguous, unsatisfying because unexplored. A discarded

version of the story continued with another ending.[15] Shiftlet returns to his "real" home, and we discover that he has
another name and is married and the father of three children. His wife announces that she has bought a television
set. Finding his children's faces "absorbed and devout like
the faces of altar boys," he picks up a baseball bat and beats
the set to pieces. Needless to say, the open end of the
printed story is preferable to the motiveless violence that
serves no end, and O'Connor wisely cut the extension.
However, her irony was not powerful enough to overcome
a negative character *and* a negative environment. The
phrase "continued slowly to descend" anticipates the ending of "The Enduring Chill" where the Holy Ghost "continued, implacable, to descend," and perhaps both endings
suffer because O'Connor tries to bring God down to man
and not man up to God. Her controlling metaphor of *rising*,
that she found reinforced by Chardin, provided her with the
uplifting endings of "Revelation" and *The Violent Bear it
Away*, as well as the title "Everything that Rises Must Converge." Whereas simile can help us to understand and to accept the existing world, only the poet's metaphor can show
us how to rise beyond both the world and our phenomenal
selves.

In "Revelation," O'Connor brought together the two
means she found for dealing with endings: irony, which
Wayne Booth characterizes as "essentially subtractive" in
that it "always discounts something"; and metaphor which
always *adds* to our knowledge of the world.[16] Nevertheless,

---

[15] Included in the Flannery O'Connor Collection at Georgia College.
[16] Wayne C. Booth, *The Rhetoric of Irony* (Chicago: University of Chicago
Press, 1974), pp. 23-24, and elsewhere. Booth includes O'Connor's "Everything
that Rises Must Converge," provides a critical reading, and discusses some problems of interpretation (pp. 152-69).

the ending again presented her with formal problems, or more precisely language questions: if irony limits us, does metaphor also have its limits? Must aesthetic order finally bow to some higher order? Is human language inadequate to express being?

The early section of "Revelation," before Mrs. Turpin gets hit in the eye by Mary Grace's book, revels in ironic detachment, and the reader is both amused by the satire, and pleased to share the author's superior viewpoint. O'Connor employs her humor as devastatingly as in any story, but by exposing Mrs. Turpin's self-satisfaction and pride, the writer may have concealed designs on the reader. As Kierkegaard wrote, irony may choose "the simplest and most limited human beings, not in order to mock them, but in order to mock the wise."[17]

We ourselves, then, may be the "community" represented by Mary Grace's mother and Ruby Turpin, and the ugly Mary Grace and the repulsive white trash are allied in their refusal to accept our values. They are the ones who never smile or laugh, a sign that they refuse to assent to generally accepted patterns of behavior. An agent of prophecy, Mary Grace acts by throwing *Human Development* at Mrs. Turpin, but her *words* (her violent metaphor) are what profoundly wound: "Go back to hell where you came from, you old wart hog." After Mrs. Turpin's physical pain has been forgotten, the words continue to fester: a metaphor has initiated a process of self-evaluation. Mrs. Turpin's questions—"How am I a hog?" and "Exactly how am I like them?"—could be answered in terms of overt resemblance: you are fat; therefore, you resemble a hog. However, Mary Grace's metaphor is not a mere simile, containing some ver-

[17] Søren Kierkegaard, *The Concept of Irony*, trans. Lee M. Capel (New York: Harper and Row, 1965), p. 268.

ifiable truth. As Mrs. Turpin wrestles with possibility, she begins to be conscious of the inadequacy of referential language. Mary Grace did not say, "You look like a hog"; her command was: "Go back to hell where you came from, you old wart hog." This hog is not a hog but a *hog from hell*, a metaphor that brings to life sublimated wrongdoing, unapproachable by means of physical resemblance. When Ruby roars at God her final "Who do you think you are?" she begins to know the Ruby Turpin that she has concealed behind various social disguises. Her question, like any metaphor, contains its echo, its answer: "The question carried over the pasture and across the highway and the cotton field and returned to her clearly like an answer from beyond the wood."

Mrs. Turpin's social accommodations have given her stability, but once her chain of being is broken by an outrageous figure of speech even her vision becomes distorted so that she sees everything *as if* it were other than it is. She sees through, not with, the eye. However, what she discovers is not the truth, but an appearance of truth, the poet's language which is both true and untrue at the same time. Even as Mrs. Turpin's utilitarian language deserts her ("She opened her mouth but no sound came out of it"), O'Connor's metaphors begin burgeoning, and the story reaches an illuminating close in which metaphor penetrates the world's surface and we see not things but "into the life of things."

> Then, like a monumental statue coming to life, she bent her head slowly and gazed, *as if* through the very heart of mystery, down into the pig parlor at the hogs. They had settled all in one corner around the old sow who was grunting softly. A red glow suffused them. They appeared to pant with a secret life.

Ruby's "coming to life" indicates that her old way of ordering experience has been shattered and that she has found access to her own "secret life." The created world has been shown to be a creating world.

This insight into nature and self could have been a perfectly satisfying ending for "Revelation," harmonious and aesthetically pleasing; but hungering for a vision that reaches beyond the borders of earthly analogy (eating all the loaves and fishes *after* they were multiplied), O'Connor gives Mrs. Turpin a vision that breaks aesthetic decorum. Looking up from the quickened natural world, she sees a purple streak in the sky, and "a visionary light settled in her eyes." In her transcendent vision, she sees not *as if* (even the fictional bridge is burned) but *as*, and the verb *to be* reinforces the "reality" of the vision:

> She saw the streak *as* a vast swinging bridge extending upward from the earth through a field of living fire. Upon it a vast horde of souls *were* rumbling toward heaven. There *were* whole companies of white-trash, clean for the first time in their lives, and bands of black niggers in white robes, and battalions of freaks and lunatics shouting and clapping and leaping like frogs. And bringing up the end of the procession *was* a tribe of people whom she recognized at once as those who, like herself and Claud, had always had a little of everything and the God-given wit to use it right. She leaned forward to observe them closer. They *were* marching behind the others with great dignity, accountable as they had always been for good order and common sense and respectable behavior. They alone *were* on key. Yet she could see by their shocked and altered faces that even their virtues *were* being burned away [my emphasis].

The ironic viewpoint which earlier united O'Connor with her reader, in deference to Mrs. Turpin, has also been burnt away, so that the vision is not only all-encompassing but unmediated. Like all Romantic flights of imagination, however, the vision must fade and the poet must come back to the prosaic quotidian world: the rail of the hog pen, the faucet that needs to be turned off. But Mrs. Turpin does not return to a world without metaphor since she has discovered, in looking down into the pig pen, a world in a grain of sand. Nature and her imagination have collaborated in defining "life." With a short coda, O'Connor grounds vision but does not diminish its companionable power:

> In the woods around her the invisible cricket choruses had struck up, but what she heard were the voices of the souls climbing upward into the starry field and shouting hallelujah.

In "Revelation" O'Connor recognized that she had reached the limits of her language resources, that her verbal energy had created an ending at once closed and open, and a rhetoric that undermined its own logic, its own ability to conclude. The ending, combining both her strategies—through irony implying detachment from a necessary power and through metaphor demonstrating its existence—stands as her culminating engagement with literary form. It was not likely to satisfy those embarrassed by the supernatural, those looking for a well-wrought urn. An editor suggested that she leave out Ruby's vision, and O'Connor wrote to her friend: "I am not going to leave it out. I am going to deepen it so that there'll be no mistaking Ruby is not just an evil Glad Annie. I've been battling this problem all my writing days." She is a good woman, not hard to find, but hard to recognize, because the good is always "something under construction." What Ruby Turpin will do or become after her revelation does not concern us because her community has been redefined as a "vast horde of souls rumbling toward heaven." What she *does* has been superseded by what she *is*.

Flannery O'Connor completed "Revelation" shortly before entering the hospital to begin her final bout with lupus, and she apparently wrote the story with relative ease. Although from her sickbed she expressed her habitual uncertainty ("I have no idea whether it works, particularly the last paragraph"), by the end of the month she was happily confident, "pleased, pleased, pleased." Despite her uncertainty in deciding whether Ruby Turpin's vision should be in the world or out of it, O'Connor knew that she had produced some of her very finest writing.

Let us bless the freak; for in the natural
evolution of things, the ape would perhaps
never have become man had not a freak
appeared in the family. — NABOKOV

AFTERWORD

In company with other Southern writers, notably the Agrarians, who aspire to embrace a lost tradition and look on history as a repository of value, Flannery O'Connor seems a cu-
rious anomaly. She wrote of herself: "I am a Catholic
peculiarly possessed of the modern consciousness, that Jung
describes as unhistorical, solitary, and guilty." Likewise her
characters comprise a gallery of misfits isolated in a present
and sentenced to a lifetime of exile from the human community. In O'Connor's fiction, the past neither justifies nor
even explains what is happening. If she believed, for example, in the importance of the past accident that maimed Joy
in "Good Country People," she could have demonstrated

how the event predetermined her present rejection of both human and external nature; but Joy's past is parenthetical: "Mrs. Hopewell excused this attitude because of the leg (which had been shot off in a hunting accident when Joy was ten)." Believing that humankind is fundamentally flawed, O'Connor spends very little time constructing a past for her characters. The cure is neither behind us nor before us but within us; therefore, the past—even historical time itself—supplies only a limited base for self-discovery.

The little attention O'Connor gives to society at large suggests that community, like history, is not central to the process of self-discovery, to the inward being that makes us independent of even our phenomenal selves. Her rare references to a larger world outside the limited arena in which a story takes place, and her few characters engage, only underscores the insignificance of established communities in her design. In "The Displaced Person," for instance, "Mrs. McIntyre found that everybody in town knew Mr. Shortley's version of her business and that everyone was critical of her conduct." The very existence of an "everybody" and an "everyone" strikes me as both peculiar and hard to credit; and whenever O'Connor portrays collective life it lacks individuals, as in the poolroom scene in "Parker's Back" in which "the big man said" or "the fat man said" or "some one said" or "some one yelled." Parker, of course, refuses to get personally involved with any group; but he is forced into a fight during which "two of them grabbed him and ran to the door with him and threw him out." It is only at this point that O'Connor's metaphor, her *as if*, can grant Parker his proper context:

> Then a calm descended on the pool hall as nerve shattering *as if* the long barnlike room were the ship from which Jonah had been cast into the sea.

In *The Violent Bear it Away*, moreover, the young Tarwater discovers his adversary relationship with the human community only after he discovers his mythic community with the multitude eating the loaves and fishes. As a prophet, Tarwater not only rejects people, but feels compelled to shatter their contentment. In the last lines of the novel, we find both Tarwater's and O'Connor's calling: faces "set toward the dark city, where the children of God lay sleeping." The poet-prophet must wake those sleeping children, her readers, alienate them from their community solidarity and expose them to the pains of consciousness. The prophet's arrival announces the end of euphoria. If both comedy and tragedy bring an audience to the satisfying awareness of some social order external to themselves, to some accord between individual and group, O'Connor's fiction displaces the individual from all that he already knows.

An earlier title for her very last story, "Judgement Day," was "An Exile in the East," but the change only underscores the limited value of geography, of "place," in O'Connor's design. Between our solitary birth and our solitary death, we engage in the insubstantial diversions the community provides, but only our solitary, realizing vision can rescue us from the poverty of fact, of a world without mystery. By short-circuiting the current running between an individual and his social world, O'Connor sends imaginative energy upward, freeing it from the confining forms of both belief *and* denial. The visionary company O'Connor joins finds its most overt evocation in the ending of "Revelation," when Mrs. Turpin stops conceiving of the streak in the sky as "an extension of the *highway*" and instead sees it "as a vast swinging *bridge* extending *upward* from the earth through a field of living fire" [my emphasis], and in the ending of *The Violent Bear it Away* when young Tarwater realizes that "nothing on earth would fill him," that only his solitary vision can connect him with his true history and community:

> He felt his hunger no longer as a pain but as a tide. He felt it rising in himself through time and darkness, rising through the centuries, and he knew that it rose in a line of men whose lives were chosen to sustain it, who would wander in the world, strangers from that violent country where the silence is never broken except to shout the truth.

Both visions fade, and the characters must return to their existing selves, but Mrs. Turpin and Tarwater will never be the same. And, having lost its priority, their world will never be the same.

Both Mrs. Turpin and young Tarwater are "chosen" and as a consequence made "strangers" to the values of society, represented by O'Connor as "good order and common sense and respectable behavior." The "revelation" that both characters share with the reader is purchased at a terrible cost: not only the loss of a familiar social order but also the loss of accustomed ways of seeing natural order. Like Kafka and Flaubert and Joyce, O'Connor makes metaphor central to narrative, but her "violent means" work toward one end, telling her audience what it does not want to hear: that no amount of social renovation can renovate the individual self, that other people can entertain and comfort us but cannot join us in the process of discovering what may be. The human heart can be enlarged, Flaubert said, only by being lacerated.[1]

Thus O'Connor displaces her readers from the middle

---

[1] Gustave Flaubert, *Letters*, ed. Francis Steegmuller (Cambridge, Mass.: Harvard University Press, 1980), Vol. I, p. 63.

ground (the social world) where prose fiction usually resides, and consequently provokes a submerged antagonism from one kind of reader, not a violent antagonism but one that more often assumes the form of dissatisfaction, uneasiness, or perhaps distaste. Just as the "prosaic" reader looks on history as an arrangement of facts, he may look on fiction as the entertaining art of making beginnings and ends meet without any radical personal displacement on his part. Tarwater struggles hard to avoid "the threatened intimacy of creation," because it leads to no satisfying resolution. A prosaic reader, described by Owen Barfield, likewise resists that threat:

> For the pure prosaic can apprehend nothing but *results*. It knows nothing of the thing coming into being, only the thing become. It cannot realize *shapes*. It sees nature—and would like to see art—as a series of mechanical rearrangements of *facts*. And facts are *facta*— things done and past.[2]

O'Connor, like any true poet, looks on the outward world of created things only as materials that a creative power activates and shapes. In nature, opposites partake of each other, in a dynamic creating process, and art serves to imitate and further the process. Therefore, no description merely describes: "The birds had gone into the deep woods to escape the noon sun and one thrush, hidden some distance ahead of him, called the same four notes again and again, stopping each time after them to make a silence." Both the song and the silence must be *made*, and "beauty" exists not in any concrete object but in the coming together of opposites,

[2] Owen Barfield, *Poetic Diction: a Study in Meaning* (Middletown: Wesleyan University Press, 1972), pp. 168-69.

only momentarily reconciled. The counter-factual language of metaphor was O'Connor's means of releasing the mind from the confines of both time and space.

As I have tried to show, O'Connor's representations of violent acts are figures of speech, not mirrors of external reality, and obviously must be read differently from those of fellow Georgians Carson McCullers and Erskine Caldwell. In a collection of Caldwell's stories, *Kneel to the Rising Sun*, a white policeman shoots a defenseless black, a poor father murders his own child who continually asks for food, a rich man's car runs down an unemployed worker, a grandfather is eaten by hogs. But the stories are documents of social protest, and the violence serves a reforming rather than a transforming purpose. The author wants to cure social ills, rid the world of poverty, injustice, economic exploitation. The community does not have to be radically displaced, only renovated. And the means is at hand: a sharpened social conscience. Even a superior writer who strongly affected O'Connor, Nathanael West, employs violence in a way that implies an available corrective. The disillusionment and boredom from which West's "freaks" suffer cause them to feed their sensations on violence. His characters learn their violence from newspapers and movies; they copy what they cannot imagine. As a result of a debased materialistic culture, West's people are "stirred by the promise of miracles and then only to violence."[3] A humanist, West would turn a mob into a community; a visionary O'Connor would recreate society, turn it into something infinite and holy.

By emphasizing one aspect of O'Connor's fiction for study—her visionary poetics—I have consequently slighted other aspects that have gained deserved admiration: her

[3] Nathanael West, *The Day of the Locust*, in *The Complete Works of Nathanael West* (New York: Farrar, Straus and Cudahy, Inc., 1957), p. 420.

irony, her satire, and, most appealingly, her incisive humor. However, other works now exist that explore the full range of her achievement. I have tried to share in her process of making, discovering rather than imposing my thesis. Although O'Connor labored to make aesthetically satisfying literary objects, she was at the same time compelled to startle her audience into an awareness that overwhelms categories such as prose and poetry, novel and short story, categories which remain conceptions of the analytic mind and inferior containers for imaginative vision. At all times I hope I have respected O'Connor's paradoxical dictum that "fiction can transcend its limitations only by staying within them." Criticism, on the other hand, has far greater limitations and even less chance of transcending them. Nevertheless, it can, I hope, make O'Connor's audience aware of the creative movement that she shares with her characters, an interior movement toward Being, beyond the world of created things.

Metaphor was O'Connor's instrument for accommodating transcendent vision to the traditional materials of prose fiction, and if in the end the marriage was unable consistently to dissolve different shapes into a composite whole, her raids on the inarticulate remain among the most powerful in contemporary literature. Perhaps it was language itself and not mortality that finally defeated her, for, as Heidegger said, "Man acts as if he were the shaper and master of language, while it is language which remains mistress of man."[4] Just as O'Connor accepted the boundaries of fiction, she acknowledged her own personal limitations. She wrote a year before her death: "I've been writing eighteen years and I've reached the point where I can't do again what I

[4] Martin Heidegger, quoted by George Steiner as an epigraph to *After Babel*.

know I can do well, and the larger things that I need to do now, I doubt my capacity for doing." Unlike writers such as Conrad who promise a revelation they never deliver, O'Connor worked throughout those eighteen years to make "mystery" visible through language, just as she apparently found it revealed in her everyday surroundings. Her theological assumptions, to my mind, placed no restrictions on her imaginative vision, for she remained the poet Sidney describes in his *Apology*, "not labouring to tell you what is or is not, but what should or should not be."

INDEX

Aquinas, Saint Thomas, 56
Aristotle, 55
"The Artificial Nigger," 16, 20, 22-
    23, 33, 46-47, 48, 58, 66, 67,
    68, 72, 73, 76, 136
Asals, Frederick, 17-18
Augustine, 34, 111

Barfield, Owen, 157
Bishop, Elizabeth, 11
Blake, William, 7, 8, 14, 65, 83-
    84, 90, 92, 96, 108, 111, 129,
    139-40
Booth, Wayne C., 147
Burns, Shannon, 114

Caldwell, Erskine, 54, 158
Carver, Catherine, 128
Chaucer, Geoffrey, 144
Chekhov, Anton, 63, 120, 126
Christopher, Georgia, 79
"A Circle in the Fire," 30-33, 35,
    39, 78, 124, 140
Coleridge, Samuel Taylor, 6, 12,
    13, 14, 52, 55, 57-58, 69, 95,
    97, 107, 125, 140
"The Comforts of Home," 10, 89,
    145
Conrad, Joseph, 53, 76, 113, 160

"The Displaced Person," 38-39,

PRINCETON ESSAYS IN LITERATURE

September 1985

The Orbit of Thomas Mann.
By Erich Kahler

On Four Modern Humanists:
Hofmannsthal, Gundolf, Curtius, Kantorowicz.
Edited by Arthur R. Evans, Jr.

Flaubert and Joyce: The Rite of Fiction.
By Richard Cross

A Stage for Poets: Studies in the Theatre of Hugo and Musset.
By Charles Affron

Hofmannsthal's Novel "Andreas."
By David H. Miles

Kazantzakis and the Linguistic Revolution in Greek Literature.
By Peter Bien

EDWARD KESSLER is Professor of Literature
at The American University, Washington, D.C. He is
the author of *Images of Wallace Stevens* and *Coleridge's
Metaphors of Being*.

LIBRARY OF CONGRESS CATALOGING-IN-PUBLICATION DATA

Kessler, Edward, 1927-
Flannery O'Connor and the language of apocalypse.

(Princeton essays in literature)
Includes index.
1. O'Connor, Flannery—Criticism and interpretation.   2. Apocalyptic
literature—History and criticism.   I. Title.   II. Series.
PS3565.C57Z725   1986   813'.54   85-43293
ISBN 0-691-06676-0 (alk. paper)